HAWAII'S NIGHT MARCHERS

HAWAII'S NIGHT MARCHERS
A History of the Huaka'i Pō

Lopaka Kapanui & Tanya Kapanui

KUKUI⌾PUBLISHING

ISBN: 9798987821206

Cover design by: Alika Spahn Naihe
Printed in the United States of America

For our children and grandchildren. No be scared.

FOREWORD

October 23, 1988 is a day I will never forget, the day I lost my Uncle Elmer Keahi to cancer.

I was overwhelmed with guilt for unexplainably choosing not to visit the man whom I saw as my father figure, in a time when he needed me most, his final days.

On the eve of his services, I tossed and turned in bed, struggling to find peace, knowing that I was less than 12 hours away from helping carry his casket to his final resting place at the National Memorial Cemetery of the Pacific at Punchbowl.

Then, in the darkness of the night, it happened. Uncle Elmer stood before me, smiling, and he gently said, "Duke, enough already. Let it go. Please take care of Auntie Rosie for me." At that moment, an exhilarating bolt of energy went through my body, from head to toe. Then he was gone.

The following day, as the family prepared for the military funeral honors, Auntie Rosie calmly walked up to me and quietly whispered in my ear, "Uncle came to see you last night. Enough already. You know you have the gift. Listen."

I knew what she meant. This was not the first time. I also understood the immense kuleana, responsibility, that came with the gift of seeing and hearing what others do not or at least choose not to believe.

Some thirty-plus years later, I would meet a special Hawaiian, master storyteller and cultural practitioner, Lopaka Kapanui, and immediately knew, he too had the gift and he too, understood the kuleana that came with it.

Our friendship quickly grew and strengthened, as did our respect for each other and trust in each other. It was uncanny how we thought alike and often knew what the other was thinking. I knew the connection stemmed from similar upbringing and the lessons taught to us as children by our kūpuna, our elders.

Lopaka's family history, traditions and customs were passed down through moʻolelo, or as he calls it, "from mouth to ear." He soaked up all that his mom, auntie and other kūpuna shared during his childhood summers on Hawaiʻi Island and Maui. I did the same, listening intently to my tutu wahine, grandma, during my childhood summers on Kauaʻi.

Lopaka learned about the importance of intent, traditions and prayer, and why night marchers only appeared during a particular moon phase, while I learned about culture and respect, and the correct way to pick ʻopihi and limu and "take only what you need."

All that said, I must admit, when Lopaka and Tanya Kapanui asked me to review their book, Hawaiʻi's Night Marchers: A History of the Huakaʻi Pō, and offered me the opportunity to write its foreword, I hesitated. The story of Hawaiʻi's ʻoiʻo is one I have respectfully spoken little about. In our ʻohana, family, we were taught early in life about proper protocol and what to do if we heard sounds of pahu drums and chanting coming from the mountains. It has always been one of those, "Don't talk, just act. Do not say, just show. Don't promise, just prove," subjects in my life.

Then I stopped and reminded myself, who was making this request. My hesitation vanished and replaced with humility and humbleness, honored by their trust. I knew if anyone on planet Earth understood the importance of integrity, truth and kuleana about this sacred subject, it was Lopaka Kapanui.

I read the dedication page, "For our children and grandchildren. No be scared." I locked in from the opening paragraph, and with every turn of the page, I found myself learning something new. The lessons continued until the final page. I literally read the entire book in one sitting and I will not be surprised if you do, too.

In this day of the Internet, sensationalism and misinformation, it was refreshing to read fact. Truth. Honesty. Yes, Google, Yahoo and other search engines have made our lives easier, but easy does not mean better, especially when it comes to a topic that is kapu, sacred and holy.

"E mau ana ka 'ike," was what Lopaka's mother and auntie would always say at the end of each lesson, "The knowledge must continue."

This book is more than just a source of credible information. I believe it is a literary gift. Mahalo nui loa Lopaka and Tanya, for understanding the true meaning of kuleana and for sharing this contribution with the world. You are fulfilling your kūpuna's wishes of continuing knowledge.

Ron Mizutani
President & CEO PBS Hawai'i
Former KHON2 News Reporter/Anchor

TABLE OF CONTENTS

Introduction

From Lopaka:

For a while now, I have wanted to put the night marcher stories I've been told into one collection. So, at the behest of my wife, I began writing them out, and then we thought, why don't we take it a step further and include the research we've done on the night marchers to create a compilation of their history?

We realize that putting this together may also help dispel much of the misinformation we've encountered over the years. Of course, the fact that the stories of Hawaii's night marchers stem from our oral traditions presents a challenge when faced with the question, "Who is right?" But we'll get to that in a bit.

I must state here that I cannot and do not lay claim to the entire oral history of Hawaii's 'oi'o. I am just one Hawaiian man who, along with my wife, has chosen to compile the information we have researched and received into one volume. I rely greatly on the word of those who claim witness to the night marchers and trust that their recollections are true.

In this age of the internet and instant downloads, one can find information about almost anything. With the deluge of data that pops up after a simple internet search, it can be quite difficult to tell fact from fiction.

A quick Google search for the history of Hawaii's night marchers will bring up several different websites with much of the same copied and pasted content. Of course, the authors for a few of those websites will change a few words around, so it doesn't look like blatant copying, but the information is often the same, nonetheless.

Therein lies the problem. With so much copied and pasted information, it's difficult to say what is correct, and as it turns out, much of the information copied is not. For example, in your internet search for "night marchers," you'll often find several of the same or similar passages stating the following:

"Since Hawaiian was only a spoken language at the time of western contact, the first written account of the night marchers was by Captain Cook in 1883. He described various sightings of ghost soldiers led by the spirit of King Kamehameha the Great pacing angrily about on the Big Island of Hawaiʻi."

Any Hawaiian historian would cringe at the paragraph above, but to people living outside of Hawaiʻi or those who don't know our history, it seems like it could be true enough, right? For those unaware, I offer a very brief lesson.

Captain Cook arrived in Hawaiʻi in 1778 and died a little over a year later in 1779. During Cook's time in the islands, Kamehameha had not yet become the first king to rule Hawaiʻi, which happened in 1810, and he didn't die until 1819. So it would have been impossible for Cook to view the phantom army over a hundred years after his own death, much less witness the night marchers led by the spirit of Kamehameha, who died many years after Cook himself.

It's impossible to say who posted the information online first. Still, I believe the original poster may have misread a paper by Katherine Luomala, an American anthropologist. She produced over 150 articles and monographs, including *Phantom Night Marchers In The Hawaiian Islands* for *Pacific Studies*, in 1983. Her paper states the following:

"They evolved in a cultural matrix that encompassed information passed on orally or from publications about nonphantom—and even some spectral—Hawaiian daytime and nighttime processions of the late eighteenth and early nineteenth centuries following Captain Cook's arrival in 1778."

And then in the middle of the following paragraph:

"The first published reference to an 'oi'o that I know of was in 1883. It stated that a phantom army led by King Kamehameha's spirit had been seen on Hawai'i."

Luomala's paper is the only source that we've found that discusses both the information about Cook's arrival and the first published reference to the 'oi'o in 1883 within a few paragraphs of each other.

The erroneous information copied and pasted across the internet is not the only information incorrectly borrowed from Luomala. In September 2016, a producer of a television show on a popular cable channel approached me. She was interested in doing a spot regarding night marchers that march through 'Iolani Palace. Specifically, she wanted me to talk about "Kamehameha leading the night marchers through Nu'uanu Valley the night Queen Kapi'olani died" and then suggested that "we" tie that to 'Iolani Palace since the Queen was imprisoned there. I told her that all of her information was wrong, and she insisted that it wasn't and tried her best to convince me that she had written proof. As it turns out, the woman's proof and her entire episode relied wholly - and incorrectly - on Luomala's paper and getting someone to agree to her script on camera.

I explained to the young producer that she should read the paper again. Luomala stated, "Kamehameha's giant spectre leading an army of kings and chiefs was also seen the night before Princess Likelike died. They marched silently through Nuʻuanu Valley, Oʻahu, going to escort the spirit of the princess (who died February 2, 1887) to the afterworld."

Luomala never mentions Queen Kapiʻolani in her paper, and it was Queen Liliʻuokalani that was imprisoned in her set of rooms on the second floor of ʻIolani Palace. The production seemed doomed from the beginning, and the spot never made it to national television.

Some websites say that the night marchers will chase you and kill you, that they are the souls of relatives who die gruesome, unexpected, or tragic deaths and remain in our world to cause mischief, and that they are the ghosts of warriors tasked with hunting down the descendants of their enemies and anyone else who crosses their paths. We even found a blog post that describes an encounter of the ʻoiʻo as "jungle warriors dressed in grass skirts." For clarification, Hawaiian warriors did not wear grass skirts.

One Wikipedia contributor changed the entire article on the Wikipedia Night Marchers page, describing the ʻoiʻo as if they were characters in a video game, stating that, for the offense of looking upon a sacred body part of a chief, "bolts of intense light and flaming heat originating from several of the warriors' eyes aimed toward the mortal. The violating mortal is incinerated instantly, and the bodily remains dissipate as vapors."

Misinformation like this in an online forum is easily copied and disseminated as fact, and people believe it. Night marchers chasing and killing someone, warriors who died tragically remaining in our world to cause mischief, hunting the descendants of their enemies, and shooting flaming heat from their eyes, incinerating their victims... After more than twenty years of studying this subject, I have found nothing in writing or in our oral traditions that suggests that any of this is true.

The stories that we've been told by our kūpuna and the stories we read from our scholars tell us that while some of the details about the night marchers may differ, the underlying information is basically the same. In documented oral interviews of kūpuna, the message is often the same; the huakaʻi pō were just a way of life. As witnesses to the night marchers, they were not afraid because they knew to stay out of the way.

As a young man, I sat at the knees of my mother, Angeline Kapanui, and my Aunty Ella Kalawa Alcon as they imparted the wisdom of their kūpuna unto me. I learned from these esteemed women that our Hawaiian traditions are our own, meaning that we, our family, do not speak for all Hawaiians. So, the stories she shared with me and the stories I tell about our family and lineage won't always be the same as those of another family from another village or island.

This presents a challenge when conducting historical research on oral traditions. Hawaii's history was passed down from one generation to the next through haʻi moʻolelo, hula, and ʻoli. As years and decades pass, times change, and so do the storytellers. Because of this, the details of the stories sometimes change as well.

Witnesses to an event may spread out geographically and end up narrating slightly different versions of the same event, which get passed along as they carry the stories forward. Subtle changes to an account over time also happen when the teller of a story makes slight adjustments to fit the area or time in which he shares the story. Sometimes, the changes are unwitting as the tale gets altered to follow the narrator's understanding of the event. These facts reflect what I learned from my mother in that the stories and traditions of my family from Kailua-Kona on the Big Island may differ from those whose ancestry hails from Hana on Maui or Hanapepe on Kaua'i.

To make matters even more challenging, 'ōlelo Hawai'i, the Hawaiian language, is a poetic language whose mo'olelo are often thick with kaona or double meanings. As a result, translations of these stories may differ, depending upon the storytellers and their personal understanding of the context.

After Western contact, once the thoughts and oral traditions of Hawaiians were finally written down, we have been able to offer more than a verbal footnote of reference. When sharing stories, I still depend significantly on first-hand experience. Yet, through research, I can refer to scholars like Mary Kawena Pukui, David Malo, Samuel Kamakau, and many others to confirm or corroborate a story or a legend.

So in compiling information for a book about the history of Hawaii's night marchers, the question of "Who is right?" can be answered by relying on the collective knowledge of our scholars of old, our kūpuna, and the witnesses that come forward, and then comparing the information.

With this in mind, we come to understand that when we find many references, both oral and written, to the night marchers having been seen during certain phases of the moon following the same paths they traveled in life, we tend to take this as fact as opposed to one website saying that they are murderous demons who will incinerate mortals with intense light and heat shooting from their eyes. My goal in putting this information together is to share the knowledge of my kūpuna and dispel the misinformation about our Hawaiian history.

From Tanya:

When people share their stories with us, Lopaka and I always try to listen with an empathetic ear. Whether it's ghost stories or tales about their lives, people want to be heard. They want to know that someone will listen to them without laughter and ridicule. And they want to know that there are other people out there who've experienced something similar. Knowing that one is not alone in his or her experiences can help maintain a sense of belonging and mental well-being. In many cases, those who share their stories with us are simply looking for affirmation.

There is often a stigma that follows those who say they've had some kind of paranormal experience and they become wary of sharing their tales with others. However, because of the many stories that are shared with us, we're able to say, "You're not crazy," or "You're not alone," and "I believe you."

Several years ago, Lopaka talked about compiling all the night marcher stories he's been told, and then later, we decided to put them together in a book with all the research we've learned. One day, I asked him to sort through our meager book collection and pull out all the books we have that contain night marcher stories or information, he turned and immediately pulled five books off the shelf.

I picked up a small, worn, discarded library book and flipped through it.

"That little book there has a story on page 112. It's not exactly night marchers, but you might be interested in it anyway."

That book was *Hawaiian Legends of Old Honolulu* by W. D. Westervelt. I flipped to the page and read the title, "The Ghost Dance on Punchbowl, Ka Hula o Na Aumakua."

"How do you even remember the page number?" I asked him.

His answer was a shrug and a simple, "I dunno," and he returned to pulling more books off the shelf.

This is the mind of Lopaka Kapanui, the *Kahuna Ha'i Mo'olelo*, the collector and teller of stories. He doesn't know how he remembers all the stories he's been told, he just does, he says.

The dozens of books he pulled off the shelf that night seemed quite random, and Lopaka assured me that there were more, we just didn't have them. Thus began our search. Our little collection of books soon became a bit larger, and what started as a quick compilation of stories turned into much more.

We visited the libraries, pored over online newspapers, and searched online booksellers looking for any information on the night marchers. One story or clue always led to more, and we've downloaded scores of old newspaper articles, ebooks, papers, and oral interviews recorded in cultural surveys and EIS reports.

We also wanted to explain the reason for the night marchers according to oral histories and the world of parapsychology, in addition to sharing personal accounts of their hauntings.

Focusing on experience-centered narratives, we set out to share the stories we've read and assembled. Through this goal, I developed a greater understanding and a new appreciation for Hawai'i and its culture. I hope this book brings to light facts, history, and understanding not only about the famed night marchers but also about Hawai'i as a whole. Additionally, I hope that those who have yet to share their own stories realize they are not alone.

From both of us:

We have spent years researching to provide as much information as possible regarding one of Hawaii's most enduring haunted tales and compiling the history and some of those tales into one book. We acknowledge that there is still much more information out there, and there are yet even more variations of stories than we describe in this book. However, please trust that we present this information respectfully and have made every effort to be as accurate as possible while keeping some names and specific locations private, as was requested of us.

Lopaka and Tanya Kapanui

He pō Kāne kēia, ke māʻau nei nā ʻeʻepa o ka pō.

This is the night of Kāne, for supernatural beings are wandering about in the dark.

Said of those who go wandering about at night. It is believed that on the night of Kāne, ghosts, demigods, and other beings wander about at will.

ʻŌlelo Noʻeau #908

"The first thing you will hear is the sound of the drums, distant at first, then louder. You will sense a foul and musky odor in the air — the smell of something that has died — and then see a long line of torch lights that grow larger and brighter. The night marchers give you fair warning to get out of their way."

— From *Haunted Hawaiian Nights* by Lopaka Kapanui

Chapter 1
O Wai Lākou, ka Huaka'i Pō?
Who are the Night Marchers?

'Oi'o.

Na huaka'i o ka pō.

Huaka'i pō.

Huaka'i pō Kāne.

Kukuihaele.

Spirit ranks.

Phantom army.

Shadowy men who march hither.

Night marchers.

There are several names for them, but each name refers to the same ghostly procession. The oral traditions of the much-feared night marchers have survived countless years by being passed down from mouth to ear and then by the learned art of writing and documentation. Their tales have survived the influx of missionaries and different cultures. Their stories have spread through hushed whispers during late-night storytelling around the dinner table. Their procession has been witnessed by Hawaiians and non-Hawaiians from different walks of life.

The night marchers hold us in rapt attention as their deeds are recounted over and over again throughout the years. However, the question always becomes, "Who are the Night Marchers?"

David Malo tells us that the 'oi'o comprised a great number of spirits. The term is generally used to mean a procession of the souls of the dead. By that definition, a person will never see a 'single' night marcher. Malo describes a single spirit of a living person as kākāola, while the ghost of a lone warrior would just be termed lapu or wailua.

The most common description of the night marchers' legend can come from any person who has lived in Hawai'i for several years. They are a group of warriors marching in death in a haunted procession. Their announcement strikes fear into the hearts of those who bear witness and comes in several forms; the sound of the pū (conch shell), the pounding of distant pahu (drums) getting closer, the music of the 'ohe hano ihu (nose flute), the sound of stomping feet, a line of torch lights traveling along a path. One might even feel the earth shake or catch the scent of sulfur. Some have said that they witnessed a column of mist moving across the land.

If you are in the way of the oncoming procession, you should run. If it is too late to run, you must lay prone, cover your head, and shut your eyes tight. If you know it, it would be helpful to chant your lineage and pray that an ancestor walks among the dead to speak for you.

If you have no one there amongst the ranks willing to claim "Na'u," your life is forfeit. Na'u is the Hawaiian term for "mine" that an ancestor would announce if they recognized you. With no ancestor to save you, then you may hear the call of "O-ia!" This is the order to "Let him be pierced!"

If you do not know the lineage of your ancestors, Kepelino states that your next hope is to strip off your clothing and lay flat on your back to convince those in the procession that you are mad and, therefore, have pity for you and leave you intact. One would hear cries in the procession of "Shame!" as they passed. Luomala shares that some even say you should remove your clothing and rub urine on your body so that you may repulse the huakaʻi pō.

Mysterious and unaccompanied deaths may be attributed to heart failure or some other natural cause, but it is said that kūpuna, older Hawaiians, would think of the night marchers.

Observations of the night marchers also vary depending on where and when the processions are seen. It is said that these processions of the dead follow the tastes, attitudes, rituals, and protocols that they followed in life.

If the chief in the procession enjoyed silence, the march would be silent except for the sounds of the implements carried within the march. If the aliʻi was fond of music during his procession, the sound of drums, nose flutes, and other instruments would be heard during the ghostly procession. The ʻoiʻo are continuing the sacred duties that they carried on in life.

If this is the case, it would then follow that same tradition that any person breaking a kapu as the night marcher procession passed would share the same fate as their ancestors whose life would be taken in exchange for their transgression.

In my business, I am always asked, "Are they REAL?"

In Hawaiʻi, you don't have to search long before you come across someone who has experienced the night marchers firsthand. A realtor who grew up in Maine with no other ties to the Hawaiian people, an old surfer whose kūpuna have lived on the same parcel of land as far back as they can remember, a janitor whose Chinese grandmother carried her traditions from the old country, a group of professionals in an office building in Downtown Honolulu; to these people, these witnesses, the night marchers are real. The sight of torches, the sounds of the drums and stomping, and the feeling of terror are all real to them. However, I do follow the belief of my ancestors, my kūpuna, and my mother in the thought that, yes, they are real. Read further to understand why I would think so.

☽ ○ ☾

The legend of the night marchers goes far beyond that of our kūpuna, back to the very beginning of our world. In some translations, the Kumulipo refers to the marchers of the night. Composed as a genealogical chant, the Kumulipo explains the history of Hawai'i in its more than two thousand lines. As the world so began, the chant also begins in darkness and tells the story of the emergence of almost every form of life, including that of gods and men.

Following is a section of King Kalākaua's text of the Kumulipo:

601. Hanau ka po Akua
602. O kanaka i kukuku
603. O kanaka i momoe
604. Momoe laua i ka po mamao
605. Ahinahina wale kanaka e kaka'i nei
606. Ha'ula'ula wale ka lae o ke akua
607. Ha'ele'ele ko ke kanaka
608. Hakeakea wale ka 'auwae

609. Ho'omalino ke au ia ka po kinikini
610. Ho'ola'ila'i mehe ka po he'enalu mamao
611. I kapaia La'ila'i ilaila
612. Hanau La'ila'i he wahine
613. Hanau Ki'i he kane
614. Hanau Kane he akua
615. Hanau o Kanaloa, o ka he'e-haunawela ia
     A--o
616. Hanau ka pahu
617. O Moanaliha
618. Kawaoma'aukele ko laua hope mai
619. Ku-polo-li'ili-ali'i-mua-o-lo'i-po kona muli
620. O ke kanaka ola loa o lau a lau ali'i

And below is Martha Beckwith's translation and notation:

It was the time when the gods were born
Men stood up
Men lay prostrate (the prostrating kapu prescribed for high chiefs)
They lay prostrate in the far-past time
Very shadowy the men who march hither (marchers of the night)
Very red the faces of the gods
Dark those of the men
Very white their chins (because living to old age)
A tranquil time when men multiplied
Living in peace in the time when men came from afar
It was hence called calmness (La'ila'i)
La'ila'i was born, a woman
Ki'i was born, a man

Kane was born, a god
Kanaloa was born a god, the rank-smelling squid
It was day
The womb gave birth
The vast-expanse-of-the-damp-forest was her next born
The-first-chiefs-of-the-dim-past-dwelling-in-the-cold-uplands
(Ku-polo-liʻili-aliʻi-mua-o-loʻi-po kona muli) her last born
The long-lived man of the two branches of chiefs

☽ ◯ ☾

THE GHOST ARMY OF KAMEHAMEHA I

One of the most famous tales of the ʻoiʻo, the phantom army, is that of Kamehameha I. In this 1883 statement, the first published account directly discussing phantom army, Reverend L. Lyons reported to Joseph S. Emerson that his friend, a Hawaiian man deemed trustworthy and not given to hyperbolizing facts, had witnessed the procession of Kamehameha I in Waipiʻo on Hawaiʻi Island barely a generation after the death of Hawaii's first king.

In Emerson's text, Reverend Lyons explained that his friend was walking alone on the Mahikiwaena road when he saw the ghostly company in the distance. Hiding behind a tree and filled with fear knowing that discovery would mean certain death, the man watched as Kamehameha the Conqueror along with his chiefs and warriors in an imposing military array marched silently toward Waipiʻo.

It is said that, once a year, this spectral procession of Hawaii's great king and his warriors are seen marching in silence, keeping perfect step, passing through the woods down to the Lua o Milu, the underground abode of the dead, in Waipiʻo Valley.

PROCESSIONS IN HAWAIʻI

Ceremonial processions were a part of life in old Hawaiʻi, and they were a serious matter. Wherever sacred aliʻi traveled, there was a procession to announce them and to follow. Chiefs and warriors marching off to battle wore their feathered finery of ʻahu ʻula and mahiʻole. They were followed by their families, their kāhuna, and those carrying the images of their gods. Kāhuna led ritual processions for dedication and purification. These processions happened in ceremony, in celebration, and in mourning. They were so common that there are even kiʻi pohaku (petroglyphs) that suggest men marching in a long procession.

Processions were not simple parades thrown together, inviting anyone to tag along. There were many kapu in place during these ceremonies. The fear of the night marchers most likely stems from the fear of death for breaking these ceremonial kapu.

John Papa Iʻi wrote of a particular procession for the cutting of an ʻōhiʻa tree to be used as the primary Kū image of the Papaʻenaʻena heiau during a kapu loulu luakini ceremony. This description shows an example of the severe nature of a procession. The loulu was a kapu period composed of several ceremonies to consecrate a heiau of the luakini class. During the kapu loulu, there were a number of strict regulations, and any infraction could mean death for the unfortunate rule breaker.

Kū is the god of war and chiefs. His elaborate heiau were of the luakini or poʻokanaka class, and he demanded human sacrifice for important rituals. Within these heiau, Kū is the principal image carved out of a single ʻōhiʻa log.

Before going to choose the 'ōhi'a log from which to carve the Kū image, the sacred adze, or 'olopū, which had been handed down from the forefathers of an ancient generation, was consecrated. All kāhuna present must observe their surroundings for signs and bad omens. If the night was clear and unmolested by inclement weather and no negative portents were present, all was well, and the procession could proceed.

The procession was made up of the king, the priests, the feathered gods, and their attendants carrying supplies and additional adzes. The one whose task it was to discern the proper tree for selection went up ahead as they marched to the place where the 'ōhi'a trees flourished. After him came the kahuna, followed by the king, then the bearer of the 'olopū, and then one who bore a healthy pig. Along the way, the many kāhuna following in the procession offered prayers, as was custom. Once the group reached the selected 'ōhi'a, the kahuna pressed the 'olopū against the chosen tree and offered a prayer. The pig was put to death and buried in the hole dug in front of the tree as an offering. At that time, all other kāhuna in attendance responded with lengthy prayers and chants.

Pigs were cooked, and drums belonging to the gods were sounded. All other food items which were brought as part of the procession were made ready. After the feast, the remnants were buried at the stump of the cut tree. If there was any man who broke kapu at any time during this procession and ceremony, he was killed, and his body was buried with the other items at the tree stump as offerings. The lawbreaker was known as kanaka no mau ha'alelea, which literally means a man left behind, as he was eliminated from the procession.

Described here was just one part of one phase of this kapu period, the fetching of the haku 'ōhi'a. There was much more pertaining to the kapu loulu, and within each of the phases and ceremonies, any infraction of the kapu, even the smallest mistake, would cause the death of the lawbreaker. There was great fear during the processions, and no one dared be in its path. The course of the procession was solemn, and there would be no fires lit, no talking or kapa beating to be heard. The only sound was that of the procession and the chanting within.

Considering the seriousness of a single ceremonial procession, if this same event were seen today on the slopes of Lēʻahi, it would make sense that any person present, not involved in the ceremony, should vacate the area as quickly as possible or lie face down so as not to bear witness and, perhaps, be killed for accidentally breaking the sacred kapu.

It is the general attitude among many Hawaiians that the night marchers themselves are not malevolent. They are not evil spirits bent on searching for and causing trouble to unwary victims. Instead, they are the spirits of warriors, chiefs, and gods who are continuing in death their tasks held in life. Observers are injured or killed by violating the kapu of the ghostly processions.

$$) \: O \: ($$

GODS AND MEN

From the earliest times, the tales of the night marchers have been carried on the wind in ʻoli and moʻolelo and whispers in the dark. The marches consisted of the spirits of dead chiefs and warriors, ʻaumākua, and akua, each of whom had their own march. Their purpose in life continued in death, just as their composure and laws in life also continued in death.

Chiefs, Warriors, and Daily Tasks

In ancient Hawaiian culture, your birth assured your status. There were kāhuna whose duty was to diligently research the genealogy of a woman. In Kamehameha's day, this was the Hale Nauā. Special care was taken regarding high-ranking ali'i to ensure noble offspring by not allowing them to form a first union with a commoner. Their goal was to find a partner of an unimpeachable degree. Only when the lines of ancestry were clearly established was a chiefly man or woman allowed to form a first union so that the offspring might be a great ali'i.

David Malo explains, "This was the practice of the highest chiefs that their firstborn might be chiefs of the highest rank, fit to succeed to the throne."

A most suitable partner for a chief of the highest rank was his own sister. This pairing was called pi'o. The child of a brother and sister would be a nī'au pi'o, an ali'i of the highest level. This child was so sacred that all who came into his presence must prostrate themselves. He or she was called akua or divine.

Such a sacred ali'i possessed the greatest mana, carrying the status of kapu moe, and would not go abroad by day. Hawaiians believed that the aka, a person's shadow, contained some of his mana. No common person dared commit the offense of allowing his lesser shadow to fall upon a sacred ali'i lest death be his punishment. Additionally, an ali'i of such high status could not allow his shadow to fall upon any person of lesser rank, for the powerful mana of the kapu ali'i may harm or destroy that person. A chief who had this kapu moe would mainly travel at night to avoid encountering people who were merely going about their daily routines and to refrain from causing undue interruptions. If he did travel in the daylight, a man walked before him, calling out "Kapu! Moe!" to warn all the people nearby to prostrate themselves. The items belonging to the chief were carried along behind the procession, and everyone must remain prostrate until the entire procession passed. If any person was caught standing, he was put to death.

A naha union, one between half-siblings, or a hoʻi union, one between an uncle and niece, also bore a child of nīʻau piʻo rank. However, these children either received the kapu moe or kapu noho, the sitting kapu. The rules of being in their presence were also such that breaking any of the kapu, even unwittingly, meant certain death.

As a boy, John Papa Iʻi was trained in observing the kapu noho by his mother. The proclamation of "E noho e!" was common in the court of the aliʻi, and Iʻi says this flustered newcomers, catching them unaware of the practice. The only way to safeguard oneself was to squat quickly and remove any kapa or kihei he was wearing. Additionally, if one was wearing a lei on his neck or head, he must quickly throw it away upon the kapu noho proclamation; otherwise, the penalty was death. If a person was fully clothed, the only way to save himself was to lie prostrate.

As stated in Kepelino's Traditions of Hawaii, the march of the aliʻi was conducted according to the tastes of the aliʻi for whom the procession was conducted. If the aliʻi had enjoyed silence in his life, the procession would have no sound other than that of the ʻumeke or food calabashes suspended from sticks, or the creaking of the manele, a palanquin, if the aliʻi had not been fond of walking. If an ali'i had been fond of music, the sound of the pahu, the 'ohe hano ihu, and other instruments would be heard as they marched. Sometimes, there were no lights, and the marches carried forward in darkness, and at other times there were torches, but they were not as bright as those for the gods.

Kepelino goes on to say that an ali'i with the alokapu must lead his own march. This ali'i is one whose face was so sacred that no living being, whether it was man or animal, could pass before him without being killed, and his own warriors were forbidden to precede him. On the contrary, should an ali'i possess the akua kapu, no one could follow behind him as his back was considered sacred, and he must march in the rear of the procession. An ali'i who had been well protected in life and had no rigid kapu upon his face or back would march between his warriors.

It is the apparitions of ali'i, along with their warriors and attendants, that are most commonly seen marching in the night hence the rule that you must lay down and not look, lest you be killed, and the marchers take your spirit with them.

'Aumākua and Other Beings

"As gods and relatives in one, they give us strength when we are weak, warning when danger threatens, guidance in our bewilderment, inspiration in our arts. They are equally our judges, hearing our words and watching our actions, reprimanding us for error, and punishing us for blatant offense. For these are our godly ancestors. These are our spiritual parents. These are our 'aumākua." - Nānā I Ke Kumu

'Aumākua are our spiritual ancestors. They are the god-spirits of those who passed, watching over us who are still living. Traditionally, Hawaiians would transform a deceased family member into their 'aumakua, which could assume the form of sharks, owls, mud hens, lizards, eels, and even rocks and plants. A relative that became an 'aumakua became the guardian spirit of that family.

An 'aumakua may warn of misfortune and protect from immediate danger through dreams, visions, physical manifestations, or that nagging feeling that something is wrong. For example, if you unknowingly did something wrong, your 'aumakua might send you a hō'ike a ka pō, a dream or a revelation in the night, or a hō'ailona, a sign or warning while you are awake. You would then have the opportunity to correct your mistake.

The 'aumākua might join the march of an ali'i in order to protect their living progeny who might, by chance, meet them on the road. So, should a commoner be unfortunate enough to be in the path of the ali'i, they may be saved by their 'aumākua, who also participated in the procession.

The 'aumākua also marched in their own processions, and in each district, music and chanting were included. They carried torches made of kukui nuts, which burned brightly, even on a rainy night. The 'aumākua were not confined to the night and may be seen during the day, followed by whirlwinds, one after another, in columns. The warning "Kapu! Moe!" was shouted as a warning for people to get out of the way or to prostrate themselves with eyes closed until the procession passed. Like the processions of chiefs and warriors, the marching 'aumākua also sometimes came to meet and take away a dying descendant.

Kamakau noted that in 1827, when Kamehameha III was staying at Wao'ala and Ka'ahumanu was at Maeaea in Waialua, O'ahu, they both witnessed something sparkling on the beach. Torches and lights were forbidden at night, but along the beach was a glowing light, ahi makaihuwa'a, the innumerable fires of the 'aumākua o ka pō, the divine ancestors of the night.

Other beings of the islands are said to have had their own processions as well. Martha Beckwith, in her book Hawaiian Mythology, wrote of a reference to the Ha'a people, the hairless 'ōlohe people in Kula, Maui, at a place called 'Ōma'oma'o. The Ha'a people had the mystical power of the demigods in the form of big war dogs. Some of these "dogs" were said to be in Kahekili's army.

Beckwith states, "These dog people still appear on Maui in the procession of spirits known as 'Marchers of the Night.' They look like other human beings but have tails like a dog."

Of course, when we speak of processions of other Hawaiian beings, we must mention the marches of the Menehune here as well. The Menehune are often referred to as the little people of Hawai'i. However, these are not similar to Ireland's lucky leprechauns or Europe's elves and gnomes, and other than their height, they bore no resemblance to dwarves. Many believe that while the Menehune were much shorter in stature, they were proportionately the same as their taller Hawaiian counterparts.

There is much debate regarding their exact origins, but it is often agreed that the Menehune lived in the forests of the mountains and only came out to the lowlands at night. They are described as only two to three feet tall and thickset and hairy. Mary Kawena Pukui wrote that the Mū, a banana-eating people, were a tribe of the Menehune. People of Kaua'i believe that the

Menehune stemmed from a group of wayfinders who traveled from far across the ocean and finally made Wainiha their home. The Menehune are known for their great deeds, accomplishing tasks such as building a heiau, an irrigation ditch, or a fish pond in a single night. The Menehune always worked at night, and as was Menehune law, all work must stop at the crow of the rooster whether the job was complete or not. If their work was interrupted for any reason during the night, the task was abandoned and never finished.

Menehune processions have reportedly been witnessed across the island chain. Many of these reports say that the processions were seen on the nights of the full moon. For example, in Waialua, Oʻahu witnesses say they have seen the Menehune lights, a line of the little people marching in the middle of the night carrying torches. In the neighborhoods built on the ʻEwa Plains, people find small, child-sized footprints creating a trail through their homes, going up the walls and even across their ceilings. There is also a particular procession of Menehune that make their way from Hawaiʻi Island, up the island chain, all the way to Kauaʻi on the same night each year. On Kauaʻi's North Shore, where the Menehune are said to have made their home, they walk toward the ocean and back to their village. And on Molokaʻi, the Menehune are said to sing while they march.

While there are no tales of certain death by being caught by the Menehune as a witness to their ghostly procession, I haven't met anyone who would be daring enough to test the theory.

Na Akua

The gods or akua of Hawai'i were powerful deities who maintained a combination of supernatural qualities with many of the characteristic frailties of men. Thus, they could be helpful or destructive, wise or puzzling, forgiving or vengeful. Akua could take many forms and may appear as an animal, a plant, or a rock. They could mate with mortals producing normal human beings, demigods, mo'o, or 'eho'eho, rock-like babies. An akua could also take partial or total possession of a person, a practice which we call noho.

The four major akua in Hawai'i are Kū, Kāne, Lono, and Kanaloa. After the great gods were the lesser gods, who were also worshiped, including Ma'iola, for healing, Kapo'ulakīna'u for sorcery, Laka for hula, and of course, Pele, the goddess of the volcano, and so many more. Beyond these akua were gods and manifestations of gods that are too numerous to list, with each of them having their own kuleana.

On specific nights, the march of the gods was much longer than any other procession mentioned thus far. Their torches burned a brilliant red, and their march was more sacred than that of the chiefs or the 'aumākua. Kepelino describes their parade.

"At the head, at three points within the line, and at the rear were carried bigger torches, five being the complete number among Hawaiians, the ku a lima. The gods with the torches walked six abreast, three males and three females. One of the three at the end of the line was Hi'iaka-i-ka-poli-o-Pele, youngest sister of the volcano goddess. The first torch could be seen burning up at Kahuku when the last of the five torches was at Honuapo. The only music to be heard on the marches of the gods was the chanting of their names and their mighty deeds. The sign that accompanied them was a heavy downpour of rain, with mist, thunder and lightning, or heavy seas. Their route the next day would be strewn with broken boughs or leaves, for the heads of the gods were sacred and nothing should be suspended above them."

The night of the gods is not one to be out playing the fool's game.

Other Spiritual Processions

It is also said that the night marchers appear to accept a chief or a warrior or a family member into their march upon that person's death. This means that they can appear during the night or the day. Witnesses have claimed to see figures of people dressed in modern-style clothing within the processions.

My friend, Jason Lindo, explains that several years ago, a prominent Hawaiian Kumu Hula passed away in Sacramento, California. That night, they were met with a terrible thunderstorm with heavy rain and powerful gusts of wind. Many halau members heard the pahu drums of the night marchers, while the Kumu's daughters said that they heard stomping feet stop at their house and then march away.

Similar to the night marchers' ceremonial and warrior processions are the spirits of the recent dead marching to the leina a ka 'uhane, the casting-off place of the souls. Once a month, the souls of those departed travel in a long line to the leina a ka 'uhane so that they may leap into Pō, the everlasting night. Fornander lists some of the sites noted as leina a ka 'uhane. For the people of Ni'ihau, there is a location at Kapapaki'iki'i and at Mauloku, just off the coast on Lehua island. Kaua'i souls are said to travel to Hanapepe for their departure. O'ahu's most northwestern point at Ka'ena and a point in the east at Kaimalolo facing Kāne'ohe Bay share the title of leina a ka 'uhane. Fornander notes that Manene, Moloka'i and Kahokunui, Lāna'i make up the leaping places on those smaller islands while Maui has two, which are Keka'a and the plains of Kama'oma'o. On Hawai'i Island, one may find the leaping places at Hilo, Waipi'o, and Palilua.

Since Fornander's time, other leina a ka 'uhane have been declared, such as Polihale on Kaua'i and Moanalua, Kalaeloa, and Downtown Honolulu on O'ahu. The difference between the night marchers and the procession of souls to a leaping place would be that the Huaka'i o ka Pō may be recurring, showing themselves during certain moon phases or events, whereas the souls that travel to ka leina a ka 'uhane to leap into Pō can only do so one time. Once a person's soul makes that leap, it is impossible for it to return to the land of the living.

THE RED-EYED ONE WHO GAZES TOWARD THE HEAVENS

My sister, Nalani, said that she could see night marchers, but not as other people might have seen them from a distance as they travel along mountain ridges or river beds in the depths of night. Nalani would see the procession of warriors marching through the bedroom of her apartment in the windy city of Chicago. She would say that she often froze on the spot and could not move. By all rights of our tradition, Nalani knew that she should have been struck down dead by one of the ghostly warriors for breaking the kapu by looking at them. However, strangely enough, they appeared to move on as if they had no clue of her corporeal existence. She said that sometimes the march would go on for hours and, without fail, there were always the ghosts of people from a more modern time trailing along at the end. Those were the ghosts of the people who had most recently passed.

Nalani's apartment in Chicago became a place where expatriates from the islands could find their home away from home, especially during holidays or when they were lonely.

Those who came into Nalani's circle formed a tight bond as most of them were transgender, just like herself. Sarah, one of those Hawaiʻi ex-pats, who had only been living in Chicago for a few months, became close friends with Nalani.

Within their group, it was common practice to call in during or after a date if something went wrong or they were feeling harassed or uncomfortable. Quite often, Nalani would come to the rescue and pick up a friend whose date had not gone well.

Sarah met a man who'd initially come to do repair work in her apartment. They hit it off, and within a week, the pair were out on their first date. When Nalani hadn't received a distress call in the middle of the date, she assumed that all went well.

Sarah wouldn't call the next day or the day after that. Nalani felt something was wrong, but she was too exhausted from work to check up on Sarah. Three nights after Sarah's date, Nalani went to bed and immediately fell asleep. It was exactly three in the morning when she was jolted awake by the sound of drums accompanied by the trumpeting of the pū and the sounds of Hawaiian chanting. She coughed and gagged as the pungent stench of sulfur filled her room. The drums thundered as the spectral procession marched through her bedroom as was usual, and Nalani was powerless to do anything but watch. When the march reached its conclusion, the entire procession came to a halt. There, at the end of the line, stood the spectral shadow of Sarah. She said nothing, but her eyes smiled as if to say she was sorry and thank you.

Nalani would learn the next day that Sarah's date hadn't gone well. She was told that Sarah hadn't yet explained to her date that she hadn't fully completed her transition into becoming a woman before their passionate affections became heated. Her date became enraged and beat her mercilessly before finally strangling her and dumping her body in the river. I don't think Nalani ever recovered from seeing her friend in the march.

In one of our phone conversations, she mentioned that our grandmother would tease her about her Hawaiian name in a foreboding tone of voice, "Ka uhi i maka o na lani," which means "The red-eyed one who gazes toward the heavens."

It seemed our grandmother knew of Nalani's abilities. Nalani never got used to it, though, and she remained terrified of her visions.

"What am I observing, brother?" She said softly, "Those who are going to heaven? What if I end up seeing myself one night?"

That was our last conversation. My Aunt called a few months later to tell me that Nalani had passed away in her sleep. Her roommates found her when she hadn't come out of her room for most of the day. I sadly wonder sometimes if she'd seen herself following along on that ghostly walk. My sister was only fifty years old when she passed.

☽ ◯ ☾

Although what is stated here are the most common legends of the night marchers, there are still differing beliefs regarding the huaka'i pō.

Juliet Rice Wichman, who made her home at Wailua on Kaua'i, explained that her head cowboy was taught by his father that the night marchers passing through one's property is a good omen and is said to have watched the procession as it passed while he stood out of view.

Journalist George Mellen reported that Wainiha resident, Moses Alohikea, claimed he saw the night marchers as he was passing Lumaha'i in his car. Moses stated that he had no fear of them as he explained to those ghostly warriors that his vehicle would not harm them.

In their book, "Tales of the Night Rainbow," Koko Willis and Pali Jae Lee share different beliefs regarding the huaka'i pō on Moloka'i. Some Hawaiians there say that the night marchers' stories began with the idea that the ghosts of their ancestors would travel down from their ancient burial caves in the mountains to help with a particular project. In their day, when these ancestors were flesh and blood, they were proud warriors who refused to bow to the rule of warring, blood-thirsty chiefs. They hid in the mountains awaiting a new time of peace, only coming down at night when their assistance was needed.

Observed by Hawaiians and non-Hawaiians alike, seen by children and adults, witnessed by both daydreamers and the most level-headed professionals, the legend of the night marchers has lasted for ages. Why do people still claim to see them even during these modern times?

☽ ◯ ☾

Chapter 2
Nānā ka ʻUhane a me ka Hoʻopahulu
Observing Ghosts and Hauntings

Processions were a common occurrence in old Hawaiʻi for many different kinds of ceremonies, and the kapu surrounding many of these events were strict and quite unforgiving. Any infraction often meant death to the rule-breaker.

However, it's been over a hundred years since the last ceremonial parades of Hawaiian chiefs and warriors. So why do people still see the ancient night marcher processions today?

Many Hawaiians will tell you that not all people have the ability to see or hear spirits and that the people who don't may never perceive the night marchers. This makes sense when you consider stories like several family members reportedly hearing the drums and marching feet right outside their Mililani home, but their neighbors or even one or two people in the same household heard nothing.

Observations of the night marchers vary depending on where and when the processions are seen. However, they also vary depending on the witness. This can be attributed to psychic or paranormal experiences. Throughout history, in all cultures, people have reported experiences beyond what science or society may deem "normal." According to multiple surveys, a broad segment of the world's population reports having had at least one experience that they believe was psychic. This experience includes seeing or encountering ghostly phenomena.

I have researched and documented hundreds of accounts of night marchers, ghosts, and other paranormal phenomena in many places throughout Hawai'i, much like my boss did before me. We are not scientists or parapsychologists, but in compiling this information, one begins to see patterns in isolated events, specific areas, and individual people. However, we are not, by far, the first to document strange occurrences.

In 1848, Catherine Crowe, the English novelist and playwright, published *The Night Side of Nature; Or, Ghosts and Ghost Seers*. In her book, the author adds a well-rounded degree of stories about ghosts and apparitions. This publication was one of the first serious studies of the supernatural in which the author points out that we cannot wholly dismiss the reality of supernatural and paranormal phenomena simply because it cannot be seen or measured.

$$) \, O \, ($$

FROM PSYCHICAL RESEARCH
TO PARANORMAL INVESTIGATING

Whether or not one believes in ghosts and the paranormal, the number of eyewitness accounts of the night marchers by different people of different cultures and backgrounds cannot be denied. The night marchers' reports are too numerous and widely experienced to be shrugged away as mere hallucinations, suggestions, rumors, or fraud.

Furthermore, tales of hauntings, ghosts, and apparitions reach back to the beginnings of human memory. The scientific documentation and study of such things began as far back as the 1800s. Let's discuss, for a bit, a little history of observing ghosts, hauntings, and apparitions in general.

In 1882, the Society for Psychical Research was founded with the intent of investigating mesmeric, psychical, and spiritualist phenomena in a purely scientific spirit. The SPR believed that ghosts and apparitions are tied to psychic experiences, and the field of psychical research focused primarily on spontaneously occurring psychic events, including ghosts and hauntings.

The SPR was initially made up of professors, classical scholars, physicists, philosophers, and mathematicians. Their approach to psychical research followed their scientific ideals, patiently cataloging information from around the world. They created a methodological and administrative framework in which psychical research could be reported and debated worldwide. Determined not to be misled by tricks, illusions, and wishful thinking, the leaders of the SPR quickly learned to spot fakes in the pursuit of scientific explanations.

As psychical research later became known as Parapsychology, the primary focus shifted toward more controlled laboratory studies of psychic abilities, but the interest in investigations continued.

As a science, parapsychology is the study of psychic or psi phenomena and is concerned with connections and consciousness of the mind. Psi phenomena are defined as exchanges of information - either between living things, between living things and the environment, or influences of living things on the environment that occur without the use of the "normal" five senses and appear to happen beyond the currently accepted physical laws of nature.

The Parapsychology Association is an international professional organization of scientists and scholars engaged in the study of psi. Established in 1957, the PA became an affiliated organization of the American Association for the Advancement of Science in 1969.

A few psi topics that have gained their focus are telepathy, clairvoyance, psychokinesis, psychic healing, and precognition. The experiences of people around the world and the phenomena associated with them are the PA's subject matter. Using well-developed scientific methods, the PA determines to what extent the psi phenomena can be explained through presently understood processes. In essence, the PA promotes the scientific inquiry into currently unexplained aspects of the human experience, disseminates this information responsibly to the public and the scientific community, and integrates this information with knowledge from other disciplines.

Receptive psi is the ability to perceive ghosts and apparitions, including night marchers. This ability may be more familiar to you as ESP, Extrasensory Perception. ESP is generally defined as various abilities involving the transfer or communication of information. Knowing that a broad segment of the world's population says they have had some kind of psychic experience, it makes sense that people other than Native Hawaiians can see, hear, or feel the night marchers.

Hauntings rely on some kind of perception of information beyond our "normal" five senses, or ESP. Apparitions must communicate and interact with a person using some sort of psychic process, or ESP. Parapsychologists believe that nearly everyone has some potential for ESP. Understanding the psychic abilities of the living is essential to understanding their ability to perceive night marchers.

THE HALE NAUA AND THE HAWAIIAN SOCIETY FOR PSYCHICAL RESEARCH

The Society for Psychical Research was used, in part, as a model for King Kalākaua's group, Hale Nauā. The first Hale Nauā, during the time of Kamehameha I, scrutinized the genealogical qualifications of those who claimed a relationship to the aliʻi.

The duties of Kalākaua's Hale Nauā expanded on those of the original group. Not only seeking to revive elements of Hawaiian culture that were becoming lost over time, the King also encouraged the advancement of modern sciences, art, and literature. In addition to promoting the production of kapa, woodwork, and shellwork, the group continued their genealogical research and also focused on science, astrology, and divination. Kalākaua's Hale Nauā membership was Hawaiian, and its proceedings were carried out in the Hawaiian language. The secret nature of the society with a mixed-gender, proudly nativist membership, the Hale Nauā was a prime target for attack by leaders of the emerging economic oligarchy who attempted to discredit Kalākaua and Hawaiian royalty. Accused of kahunaism and occultism, the society ceased to exist shortly after the death of King Kalākaua in 1891.

Interestingly, just twenty-six years after the overthrow of the Hawaiian Kingdom, in December 1919, the Hawaiian Society of Psychical Research was formed with Judge Sanford B. Dole as its first president. The object of this organization was to study manifestations of spiritual life and similar phenomena. Once a month, the society would invite the general public to its meetings. Just a few years later, a Maui branch was opened as well. There are several articles in some of the older Hawaiʻi newspapers that mention the society and its investigations into local hauntings.

Skeptics may claim that psi phenomena and parapsychology do not exist, and there has never been any scientific evidence to prove their existence. In actuality, there have been almost 140 years of independently replicated experimental evidence under strictly controlled conditions that say otherwise. There is more evidence to support that psi exists than there is to say that it doesn't.

All of this information leads to studying and researching the night marcher phenomenon. These days, many people seem to believe that the terms parapsychology, paranormal investigations, and ghost hunting as interchangeable and are primarily based on what they see on television. Every week, the public at large watches a group of people venture into dark places armed with all kinds of equipment that have fancy-sounding technical names, all with the hope of capturing proof of a ghost or entity and perhaps even yelling at or calling out these spirits to "do something" in order to obtain the evidence they seek. In the span of a television show, the stars are expected to solve the riddle of what the witnesses are experiencing, find the spirit and sometimes banish it, and leave the family or business owners living happily ever after.

Real paranormal investigations are nothing like that. Actual investigations involve knowing the history of ghosts and hauntings. An investigation means researching the history of the place one is investigating and talking with the witnesses and the people involved. A paranormal investigation means delving into what might be happening in the area to cause these people distress. It's understanding the effects of the immediate environment and asking questions. Is there mold in the building? Are windows and doors a possible source of cross-breezes that would cause doors to slam and items to fall off shelves? Are there power lines nearby? How is the family dynamic?

It is important to be empathetic when speaking with witnesses. Whether or not the investigator believes them isn't the question. These witnesses are the ones who believe they had a paranormal experience. When the investigator takes his personal opinion out of the equation, the question becomes, is he able to help the witnesses understand what they've experienced?

When a person shares a ghost story or an encounter with night marchers with me, my job is to listen and document the tale. Then, if they ask for help, we research the possible causes of their experience and try to offer sensible solutions.

Paranormal investigations include hours and hours of watching and waiting for something to happen and carefully documenting everything that does happen. Most of the time, it's not glamorous at all, but through real and thorough investigative practices, men and women have been able to observe and document hauntings around the world.

Nearly 140 years of research of cases around the world tells us that there are general, differing definitions of hauntings and apparitions. Parapsychologist, paranormal investigator, and author, Loyd Auerbach, explains these in detail in his books, but we'll share only the most general descriptions here.

HAUNTINGS

A mere haunting is like a visual recording playing over and over again in a loop. You would see the same ghost in the same place, doing the same thing it always does, but it would not recognize or interact with you. The phenomenon will repeat, and others may also experience the same thing. These events are often tied to anniversaries or may be more prevalent during certain weather conditions or moon phases.

There is a story from the Downtown Honolulu Post Office in 1925 about a postal worker, Benedict Westkaemper, who committed suicide. A month later, Adam Wong, another postal worker, went to the basement to procure supplies and saw the deceased coworker walking toward him. Before Wong could get his supervisor's attention, the figure vanished, "Just like smoke," Wong said. Westkaemper, who was said to guard the government's office supplies with a zealousness that bordered on freakishness, was dressed in dark pants and a white striped shirt, just like he always wore. To this day, workers in that post office swear they've seen the ghost of that old postal worker hovering around the halls without any actual interaction with the living. So perhaps Westkaemper left such an emotional imprint in the office where he worked that his psychic impression appears, as if to continue his duties just like he had when he was alive.

While a haunting may represent events that occurred in the past, the ghosts continue as if nothing has changed, regardless of the length of time or the change in the environment, such as a new building or road.

Another example of a haunting comes from a story about a special place on the island of Kaua'i. Juliet Rice Wichman wrote of a ceremony witnessed by a Japanese man who lived nearby and occasionally did odd jobs for the family and acted as a caretaker. As Wichman put it, it was hard to imagine this man, Taka, could be subject to hallucinations and even harder to imagine he would manufacture the story he was about to tell her.

Taka lived with his family along the river's edge, further back in the Wailua River Valley. Taka's family and some friends were celebrating on Christmas Eve and settled down rather late in the evening. They were awakened by the sounds of drums and voices singing in the distance. The music made the men believe that another celebration was happening, and they decided to check it out.

Further up the valley was a meadow, and as the men drew closer to this meadow, the singing grew louder, and the drums sounded out with a clear, more distinct rhythm.

Taka described the music as distinctly Hawaiian, "like old Hawaiian-very fine singing."

At the far end of the meadow was a tall rock, roughly sixty feet in height. This "male" rock was once purportedly celebrated in legend. It stands out, rising abruptly from the level river bottom land, somewhat like an abandoned stone smokestack. Its "female" counterpart is partially submerged in the river. The music was coming from the direction of that tall rock.

The men were excited to see what was happening and watch the fun, so they crossed the meadow until they came within sight of the stone. At its base was a great gathering of Hawaiian women of all ages. According to Taka, the women were wearing "old style" dress of ti leaf skirts with green lei around their necks. A group of older women seated on the ground beat drums and sang in unison while the younger women danced a hula.

This went on for a little while as the Japanese men watched until suddenly, like a passing mist, the women faded from sight.

The men were confused, wondering if their eyes and ears deceived them. They partly realized that they weren't really watching actual people dancing and singing, but for a year, they were not entirely convinced that the Hawaiians didn't just slip away while the men weren't paying attention.

The story made its rounds among their friends, and there were many nights the Japanese men stayed up, waiting to hear the sounds of drums and voices. But there was nothing.

After a year, some of Taka's friends thought the event might occur again on Christmas eve, so around twenty men spent the evening with him, hiding in that secret spot near the tall rock. They waited and waited. And then they waited even longer. Finally, when the hour of last year's manifestation came and passed with nothing happening, the men were tired of waiting.

"They think I lie," said Taka.

Around 2 a.m., the men returned to Taka's cottage to sleep, but one man suddenly heard the splash of paddles in the river. He peered out the window and saw a strange, white canoe passing. He woke his friends, and they watched this peculiar white canoe disappear around the river's bend.

They waited a bit and could soon hear the sounds of drums and singing far in the distance. Suddenly, the men were no longer tired and rushed off to the spot they'd just left. There, they saw the same scene as the year before, the women beating out a rhythm on their drums while singing, other women dancing. Sometimes only one woman sang, and sometimes all of them joined in while the men secretly watched in wonder and enjoyment.

Wichman asked Taka, "Weren't you afraid?"

Taka replied, "Very nice music, very good dancing, very fine wahine!"

Once again, the following year, a crowd of Taka's friends assembled. While they had no sight of the strange, white canoe as the year before, they did hear the drums and the voices. Again, they were rewarded with the ghostly performance of the women.

Wichman learned later that the Wailua district was once rich with lo'i. What were once kalo patches in the valley were now rice fields. In ancient times, there used to be an annual ceremonial festival of great importance to women. A fertility rite was held in the meadow near the old "male" rock during the Makahiki season.

It matters not who is present to witness or how things may have changed since the original event. The haunting is bound to the location and will repeat the same movements, the same activity over and over, without any interaction with the living. These interactions separate a cognitive apparition from a haunting ghost.

In this way, sometimes the night marchers may be considered a simple haunting, a spectral recording, playing the same eerie loop every time the conditions are just right, especially during the anniversary of the original event.

Tales of the night marchers walking through the same condominium when the moon is in a particular phase or the grand procession of Lono circling Hawai'i Island every year at the start of the Makahiki are just a couple of examples of this, the ghostly procession continuing on without regard to what is now in their path.

APPARITIONS

The concept of an apparition is directly related to the idea of life after death. One can think of an apparition as the personality, the consciousness, the soul, however one prefers to describe it, surviving the death of our body, and it is capable of interacting with the living. A cognizant being may react to their surroundings and the people therein the same way a living person would.

In some cases, an apparition may attach itself to a person or a family, following them from place to place. Again, it's likely due to a personal or emotional connection. Indeed, in our Hawaiian culture, we believe that our ancestors' spirits are ever-present and watch over us always.

While one may associate a ghost with a particular location, apparitions may not necessarily tie themselves to only one place. It seems quite possible that, as in life, a spirit may have some kind of emotional association with more than one location and may be seen in those different places—for instance, the ghost of our great Queen Liliʻuokalani.

Queen Liliʻuokalani, the last reigning monarch of our Hawaiian nation, was the younger sister of King Kalākaua and was crowned on January 21, 1891, the day her brother's body arrived in Honolulu Harbor on the USS Charleston. Quite progressive for her time, Queen Liliʻuokalani traveled extensively, understood land and water rights, and was eloquent in expressing her opinion while speaking, composing music, and writing in multiple languages.

Her reign as queen was short as the Hawaiian Kingdom was overthrown on January 17, 1893, by a handful of American businessmen with the help of the United States Marines. Later accused of treason by the new territorial government, she was forced to abdicate the throne on January 24, 1895. She spent eight months imprisoned in the corner room of ʻIolani Palace.

Today, many people claim to have seen the queen standing at the window of her imprisonment room or roaming the interior of the palace. She has also been seen wandering about her former residence at Washington Place and the grounds of the Hawaiʻi State Capitol, which was the previous location of the palace barracks.

According to the Hawaiʻi House Blog, the office manager for a senator in the 1980s recalls an incident that happened in the Capitol building. She was working a little late into the evening, and she had her young daughter with her. Because she was waiting for her husband's call to pick them up, she hurriedly brought her daughter to the restroom and told the girl to walk back through the corridor when she was finished and to look for the lighted doorway, which was her office.

After her daughter failed to return, the woman searched the restrooms on every level and called security when her daughter could not be found. The security staff instructed the worried mother to wait in her office while they looked. Shortly after, the daughter appeared in the doorway, speaking to someone that the mother could not see. The woman rushed to her daughter but found no one else there.

Upon leaving, they passed the statue of Queen Liliʻuokalani, and the daughter said out loud, "Look, mommy, that's the lady who helped me."

It would seem that Queen Lili'uokalani may have a lingering connection to her imprisonment room in the palace in addition to where she lived out her last days at Washington Place and around what are now the grounds of the Hawai'i State Capitol. These encounters may be labeled as an apparition.

If the ghostly presence that is witnessed seems to have some intelligence or true personality behind it, it is considered to be a true apparition. However, if the presence does not display any type of interaction or self-awareness, it is usually a simple haunting, like a video recording.

The idea of the ghostly warriors killing a living person who broke the ancient kapu and the appearance of the night marcher procession upon the death of another warrior or chief seems to show an awareness beyond that of a mere haunting. There are also numerous accounts of a person being forced to lie face down by an unseen presence as their family name is whispered in their ear while the ghostly procession passed. These actions seem to show cognizant apparitions interacting with living people.

In the case of the 'oi'o, we find that they do not strictly adhere to the straightforward definitions of either hauntings or apparitions. It would seem that certain processions can be considered hauntings when they cause no disruption and harm no one but continue on their nighttime walk regardless of what may be in their way. However, it would seem that other processions would be viewed as apparitions when they call out the name of a witness or arrive to meet a dying descendant. Because the night marchers don't follow one particular rule other than being a great number or procession, Hawaii's unique and legendary night marchers stand out against a field of repetitive hauntings and cognizant apparitions.

☽ ○ ☾

Chapter 3
ʻIke Maka ka Huakaʻi Pō
Witnessing the Night Marchers

It is a common belief among Hawaiians that those departed often return to the places they knew on earth. We know that our ancestors remain with us long after they have passed. They may appear in the forms and wearing the garb that distinguished them in life and often reenact important events. The most fearful of these returning spirits are the Huakaʻi o ka Pō, the Marchers of the Night, whose most common activity is to march along the trails known to them in life. Many of these trails are still known today, their stories passed down through families and friends or witnessed by people from all walks of life.

VALIDATION

Years ago, before my daughter was dragged across the U.S. continent to the shore of another ocean, before I met my current wife, before all of this took off, I was just another guy struggling with the stresses of life, trying to make ends meet when I got a call that would change everything for me.

I was stressing out, worrying about bills and rent. I was still in the infancy of making my passion my full-time life's work, and I hadn't yet learned the true value of my craft. At the time, I had my regular ghost tours as well as speaking gigs and storytelling gigs, but the lack of consistency of those tours and events became a problem. Thus, financial and personal struggles that seemed impossible on this particular day suddenly seemed less critical because of a phone call I received. That call would turn out to be a beacon of light, piercing through a dark cloud of hopeless gloom.

The caller was an acquaintance I would see every now and again. Our interactions were always friendly, and we never failed to regard one another with gentlemanly respect. You can imagine my surprise when, upon answering the phone, there were no formalities.

"What are you doing right now?" The urgency in his voice told me that a second question was soon to follow, no matter what my answer would be.

"I'm at home trying to figure out how to do twenty things all at once," I chuckled at the ridiculousness of my situation.

"Can you come to my office right now?" There was a crack in his voice that made it sound like he was on the verge of shouting, "We ordered lunch, so it should be here by the time you arrive."

His office, like the building it was in, was unremarkable. It was one of those buildings in downtown Honolulu that you don't really notice unless you've got an address for it and an appointment inside, otherwise it just seems to lose itself in the scenery. The bland khaki and vanilla color scheme of the walls and furniture gave off a dull business-only vibe. It didn't evoke any emotion, nor did it enhance or desensitize a mood. No life, no spice, just bland. Quite contrary to the meeting itself, which was anything but dull.

We exchanged our handshakes and half hugs, and he gestured to me to have a seat at a table in the corner. A kupuna wahine entered the room with her own plate of Hawaiian food and sat down to join us. The three of us made small talk, with the main focus on our families and our jobs. Once we finished, he motioned for me to follow him to his desk, where I sat and waited for the real purpose of this meeting to be revealed.

"Tutu," he looked to the kupuna, "Do you want to show him and explain?"

"No," she replied in a sweet voice, "You may show him."

The man reached into the lower cabinet drawer of his desk, removed a long cardboard cylinder, and placed it on the desk. He pried the cap off one end and turned it upside down, and a large rolled-up piece of paper slid out. Leaning forward, he carefully spread the paper open with both hands and then placed four large paperweights on each of the four corners of the large parchment.

At first glance, I thought I was looking at some abstract drawing of an octopus-like creature with dozens of arms spreading in all directions. But, as I examined it closer, I realized I was looking at something that overlaid a large map of Oʻahu.

"What's this supposed to be?"

His half-smile seemed closer to a smirk on his face, "It's a map of every night marcher trail on Oʻahu."

The man pointed to each line without saying anything, and his gesture brought every marked line back to one common source on the map.

"They all begin from around here."

I was dumbfounded. I was covered with chicken skin, and I was shocked, and I was speechless. Oh, yes, and I was crying. He pointed to the kupuna wahine, who was still sitting at the table where we had just eaten our lunch. She looked at us with tears in her eyes. After a few minutes, the man rolled up the map and placed it back in the brown cylinder.

"This is her map," he nodded toward her, "This is countless generations of oral history regarding the night marchers on one large map."

He held it out for me to take, and I took a step back instead.

"She wants you to have it. There's no one in her family that she can pass it down to because they want nothing to do with it. They told her to burn this map and be rid of it. She knows that this will survive in your hands."

So many thoughts ran through my head at once. THIS! This is the validation I've needed to continue doing what I love. These are not just stories my mom, my boss, and many others made up. These are our oral traditions. This is our history! The anticipation was palpable. I stood there contemplating what this means; what it means to me, to my family, to my mom who told me countless tales, to my old boss who so diligently collected the stories, to every Hawaiian and non-Hawaiian witness to those phantom warriors that march in the night.

I could see myself investigating these places and documenting everything I see and hear and feel. I could see myself sharing this information with my daughter and explaining to her that her dad's really not crazy. And then.

Then I could see someone else getting a hold of this map. I could see people being disrespectful, not taking the proper precautions, and acting like everything was a joke. I could see someone getting hurt.

After staring blankly for several minutes at the spot on the desk where the map once lay while my mind raced with thoughts of validation, pride, and fear, I took a step back. I looked at the kupuna and smiled at her, and then I turned to look at my friend.

"No disrespect," I replied with my hands out to him, my heart was pounding, and I could hardly believe what I was about to say, "I don't want it."

There was a pause before I continued, "I mean that I don't want to take it, and it accidentally disappears, or someone steals it. Who knows what the wrong person might do if they ever came across something like this? As a people, we're already losing so much. Something like this... the eye of men should never behold."

"Are you crazy?" He hissed at me with disappointment, "She's handing down her life's work to YOU!"

"He's right," the kupuna wahine inserted herself into the conversation without ever having moved from her spot. "He understands the burden of caring for... for this map of our ancestors who travel in the night."

She smiled and nodded at me while the tears fell from her eyes. I walked to her and knelt at her feet, where she held me for a long while until her tears subsided, "We'll keep the map here for now until the time comes for you to care for it."

I nodded and thanked her. Then, standing up, I walked over to my friend and shook his hand. I thanked him for lunch, and then I left. Presented with the task of sharing our moʻolelo, the oral traditions of my people, this map reaffirmed my life's work and gave new meaning to my job as a storyteller. However, I don't need to share the map itself to share the stories. That particular burden of knowledge was still safe for the time being and would not be mine to bear.

☽ ○ ☾

My friend, Jason Lindo, shared a story about his grandfather, who also knew about maps that showed night marcher paths. Jason's grandfather learned to read the old Mahele maps from his aunt and uncle on Kaua'i. The following story is in Jason's words.

"My grandpa was George K. Spencer, and he retired as a city building inspector in 1968. He spoke and read Hawaiian fluently. It was his first language. He used to be called in to read the Mahele documents that showed boundaries, particularly those that were kuleana lands.

"He said you could tell the night marcher trails because they were broken lines. They did not change from survey map update to update, whereas boundary lines were solid and did change. Often, they were not straight lines. They went around certain pu'u or large pohaku.

"He was called often to look when people were building as they wanted to make sure they weren't in a night marchers' line or near one of the marchers' ala or that they oriented their doors a certain way so they could march through the house directly.

"They would also ask where to plant lā'ī boundaries to make the marchers detour around their properties. As you said, they always went from Mauka to Makai.

"If it was a marcher's line for a chief, it usually ended at the kai, but if it was for the akua, it ended at the site of a heiau.

"A lot of them went through what is now Chinatown, also places in Waikiki.

"I encountered them once in high school on Tantalus by Ualaka'a park and once while staying at a friend's beach house at Malaekahana.

"My grandpa did several times fishing out at Mokulē'ia when he would camp at night."

The night marchers have traveled not only on Oʻahu but they march to and fro on every major island in our chain. Some kūpuna will tell you that the ghostly army marches from mountain to ocean or from heiau to ocean and heiau to forest. Others say that the night marchers follow rivers and streams. All of this makes sense when we understand that the processions followed paths that they took in life, like when a sacred aliʻi traveled to the ocean, or when an ʻohiʻa log was needed to create the great statue of Kū in a heiau. During times like these, a procession was formed and commoners either vacated the area or lay prostrate as the parade passed.

The stories in this section are moʻolelo that have been posted in newspapers and printed in books written by scholars such as my old boss, Glen Grant, and many others. They are also stories shared with me by people who believe they have experienced the phenomenon of the huakaʻi pō. These are not "investigations" within the scope of the paranormal community.

I cannot reproduce the map I had the privilege of viewing or tell you exactly where all the trails are, but I can discuss some of the more common trails and general areas that people have already mentioned. Keep in mind that as the Kumulipo goes back to the beginning of Hawaii's history, so do the traditions of our people, going back hundreds of years, perhaps thousands. Listed here are absolutely not all the night marchers' paths in Hawaiʻi. These aren't even all the stories I know or have been told. Some people have asked that I not share their stories at all, while almost everyone who did consent requested that I not share their real names.

Take from this what you will, but I must caution you, if you choose to seek out the Huaka'i o ka Pō, you may not like what you find. This book is not meant to be your ghostly guidebook to ultimately finding the infamous night marchers, nor is it definitive proof that they do or do not exist. In all actions and events that you choose to participate in, your choices are your own, and you do so at your own risk.

KAUA'I

Anciently known as Kamawaelualani, the child of two heavens or two royal houses, it is the oldest in the island chain. Its hula lineage extends back to what modern kumu hula refer to as an unrecorded time. One of Kaua'i's most notable progenitors is the celebrated Prince Lohiau, known for his expertise on the pahu drum and his ethereal performance of hula.

Polihale

Located on the most western shore of the island of Kaua'i, Polihale beach is the longest sandy beach in Hawai'i. Polihale is the site of a leina a ka 'uhane, a leaping place where the souls of the dead leap into Pō, the everlasting night. At the northern end of the beach, there is also a heiau. In a state of disrepair and buried in the thicket of thorny kiawe trees and other brush, the heiau there is reportedly dedicated to Laka, the hula goddess, and was used for special ceremonies up to the time of King Kalākaua.

Now a state park, Polihale greets families and fishers, campers, and partiers with long stretches of hot, white sand and clear blue waters during the day and a darkness at night that is so complete that the glittering stars stand out, sparkling beautifully against a velvet sky. In this darkness, at the northern end of the beach, toward this heiau and this leaping place, people have witnessed the night marchers and the procession of the dead.

One fisherman stated that he made plans to camp out with some friends over a long holiday weekend. It was late on that first night of camping and fully dark, he explained, and he'd just finished checking the bait on all of his poles. The fisherman was just ready to sit down when someone exclaimed, "What is that?"

The fisherman saw nothing out of place and turned to his friend, but before he could ask the man what he was talking about, he heard what he thought sounded like drums. At first, he scoffed and believed it was a trick of the mind hearing the waves pounding against the sand. Then, suddenly, several others in the group heard it too. At this point, everyone was standing, looking around.

The fisherman said, "Brah, we were all ready to fight. We thought somebody was messing with us!"

As the sound became more rhythmic, there was no way it could be mistaken for the pounding surf. It was suddenly hot, and it felt like the air was sucked away.

Someone in the group yelled, "Night marchers!"

They all lay flat on their stomachs and covered their faces without hesitation.

"It seemed like a really long time," the fisherman explained, "But it was probably only a few minutes. We just all lay there, listening to the drums get louder and louder. Even after the sound was gone and we could feel the wind again, we were afraid to move. Total chicken skin, brah."

I asked what they did afterward, and my question was met with a laugh, "We left! We not gonna catch any fish after that, and we don't know if they supposed to come back or what. I rather go fishing another day than be hard head and something bad happens. My Tutu taught me better than that!"

Hanapēpē

Hanapēpē is well known for the endangered practice of ho'ohāhāpa'akai, gathering salt. Pa'akai from Hanapēpē, Kaua'i, is a gift that is treasured throughout the world. From time immemorial, salt makers have prepared and harvested salt in this sacred place. In recent years, this practice has been threatened by changing weather patterns, sea-level rise, and the proposed expansion of the neighboring airport.

Contesting a request for a permit to renovate Burns Field, also known as Port Allen Airport on Kaua'i, a Native Hawaiian activist and chief librarian at Waimea High School claimed that Burns Field lies in the path of the night marchers. The ancient warriors are said to travel from deep in Hanapepe Valley toward the shore, marching through Burns Field to the ocean.

Māhā'ulepū

Headed towards the Southern shore, we take the scenic route through the famous Tunnel of Trees on Maluhia Road. Aptly named, the Tree Tunnel is made up of hundreds of fragrant, century-old eucalyptus trees planted along nearly a mile of roadway whose branches seem to reach across the road creating a beautiful tunnel of shade and foliage. Many late-night travelers claim that the Tree Tunnel is haunted, but that's a legend for another book.

One will have to venture off the paved road to reach another site of the phantom night marchers, the place known as Māhā'ulepū. Away from the bustle of town, Māhā'ulepū is an important site in Hawaii's history and culture. Against a backdrop of tide pools, lava tubes, and sand dunes lie important ecological, geographical, and historical finds, including petroglyphs, native plants, and fossils of endemic fauna.

Māhā'ulepū is also a popular spot for shore fishing, and one will often see people camping overnight in hopes of catching a prized ulua. There are superstitions and precautions that every fisherman heeds; some are obviously for safety, and some are supposed to guarantee a good catch.

Among these precautions are instructions to never sleep on the trail that runs to and from the shore. Some say it's because it's bad luck, while others say that it's just a common custom that everyone follows.

Two fishermen on Kaua'i shared a cautionary tale of why this rule exists. A young man who had planned a weekend stay arrived at the fishing area after working all day. He passed the time catching smaller fish for bait and sliding them down the long lines that were thrown out as close to the offshore channel as possible. With a final check of his lines and bells, he decided to settle in and sleep for a bit. The young man, who was too tired to clear out a space to lay his sleeping bag decided that the superstition was just that and curled up in his sleeping bag right in the middle of the flat trail to catch a late-night nap.

He woke up from a nightmare just before dawn and felt aching pains throughout his body. When the sun finally rose, the young man saw what looked like human bite marks all over his body, even in the most sensitive areas.

The older Hawaiians told him that he was sleeping on the path used by the night marchers, and this was the reason they say one should never sleep on the trails at Māhā‘ulepū.

The two fishermen who told me the tale laughed heartily, "These young guys, bumbai they learn."

According to them, young man swore he'd never fish overnight there again.

Wailua

On the eastern side of the Garden Isle, before highways, sugar plantations, and the famous Coco Palms Hotel, the Wailuanuiaho‘ano (Great Sacred Wailua) complex was the place of kings. Within the vast complex were several sacred heiau from shore to mountain.

Kukui Heiau, a healing and navigational heiau, sits on the point of the northern shore of the mouth of the Wailua River. Directly across the bay is Hikinaakalā, ever-present to greet the rising sun, with Hauola, a pu‘uhonua, right next to it. A person who had violated a kapu could seek refuge at a pu'uhonua, such as Hauola, to escape punishment.

Following upriver, we have Malae, a luakini heiau, and Kalaeokamanu, also known as Holoholokū, where chiefs were born, and the nearby ali'i birthstone, Pohaku Ho'ohanau, and Pohaku Piko, a stone upon which the child's umbilical cord was placed.

Heading mauka, upon a bluff overlooking the Wailua area, including the river, the bay, and the ridges and peaks of the Wailua River Valley, we have Poliahu heiau. This luakini heiau is said to have been built by the Menehune. Located near the Poliahu Heiau is the Wailua Pohaku Kani, the Bellstone. The Bellstone is described as a reddish basalt boulder that, when struck, would produce a hollow sound that could be heard over a great distance. The Bellstone was used to announce important events such as royal births or the approach of chiefly or religious processions.

It was in this valley that Juliet Rice Wichman made her home on the mauka bank of the Wailua River and called it "Pihanakalani" after the lost home of the magical fountain Waiokeola where lived two very high chiefs, Kauakahi'ali'i and his sister Kahalelehua. One night, a few months after moving into their new home, Ms. Wichman states that their head cowboy excitedly described his night marcher encounter to her and her husband.

It was late at night. The family had already gone to bed, and the cowboy noticed that the dogs were acting particularly excited, listening to something. As he listened too, he heard the sound of old Hawaiian drums beating in the distance toward the foot of the mountains. As the sound grew nearer, the dogs became frantic. The cowboy's interest was piqued, but not his fear. He had heard from his father the tales of ghost armies that passed at night along old war trails and was told that this was a favorable omen of protection for those whose lands they passed over.

Closer still, the sound of drums came, and the dogs ran down the little valley behind his house and followed the sound up the hill, running as if they were beside a column of marching men. The cowboy said that as the drums beat louder, he could hear the stomping of feet as they passed him and began to die away in the distance.

Mrs. Wichman describes the man as "Exceedingly steady and reliable and not given to drinking."

She also explains that while it was their first time learning of the ghost army, she has personally heard them since then.

Lumahaʻi

Located on the North Shore of Kauaʻi, the picturesque beach of Lumahaʻi is well known for its beauty and its dangerous rip tides. Nonetheless, residents and visitors alike brave the long, steep hike down to the shore in search of the perfect beach day.

Lumahaʻi is also known amongst the locals for its legends. In 1940, journalist George Mellen interviewed Wainiha resident Moses Alohikea on his experience with the night marchers.

Moses stated that in the late 1920s, he was returning from Hanalei in his car around midnight. He began to cross the mouth of the valley and heard the steady beat of the pahu and the stomping feet of a thousand men. The man said that the air was warm and smelled of men. With chicken skin going up his back, he knew it was the marching ghost army of Lumaha'i. Moses then said he would have been killed if he had been walking, but he explained that he meant no harm and that his vehicle would not hurt them. He stated that he also heard women walking because they made a different sound. He made it through the crowd, happy to get through alive.

Hanalei

According to Emma de Fries, her grandfather started a rice plantation in Hanalei. One day, the Chinese laborers who worked the rice paddies said they saw hundreds of men carrying spears. They were dressed in malo and wearing short, feathered capes walking down the mountain trail. As the marching army drew closer, then workers ran in fear, stopping some distance away. They turned to look back and were amazed to see the warriors walking straight through a stone wall that was in their way. Afterward, the marching army disappeared into the Hanalei River.

☽ ○ ☾

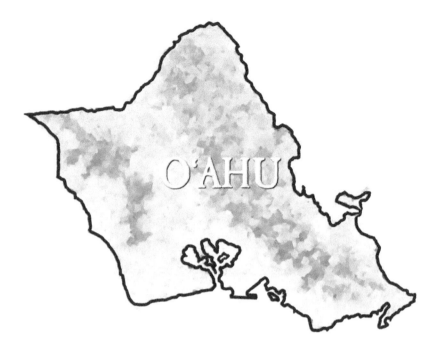

Someone asked me once, "What is the most haunted island in Hawai'i?"

I had to say, hands down, it must be O'ahu, and I still agree with this statement today. There are powerfully spiritual and absolutely haunted places on every major island in our chain, of course. However, due to the sheer number of people here and such widespread activity, there just seems to be many more instances of hauntings on this particular island.

Wai'anae

I used to take a ghost tour out to the Wai'anae coast once in a while. It was one of the remnants of my days working with Glen Grant. The most western part of our island is so rich in beauty and culture that it would take days and weeks to point out all that is worth seeing. Since I only offer a three-hour tour, I have to cut it down to three magical spots. One of those spots is Keawa'ula, also known as Yokohama Beach.

Many people have said they have witnessed a line of torch lights making their way down the mountain in an almost zigzag pattern before emerging from the tall grass headed towards the ocean. Glen used to share his night marcher encounter on his own Wai'anae tour.

In the late 1990s, Glen was hosting a college group at Keawa'ula. The students were gathered around, sitting in the sand, as a large bonfire was burning nearby, and Glen and his Hawaiian friend shared ghost stories back and forth.

After a while, the fire began to lose intensity, so Glen and his friend took a break from storytelling to gather pieces of wood from the nearby field. As he was collecting whatever sticks and pieces of wood he could find, Glen said that he looked around and saw the tall grass around him moving to and fro, but, for some reason, he couldn't feel or hear the wind blowing. It suddenly became stifling hot, and the sickening sweet stench of something dead filled his nostrils.

He reached out and tapped his friend on the shoulder and asked, "Do you see this? What's going on?"

The Hawaiian man stood up straight and looked around. Witnessing the same phenomena as Glen, the man remarked, "Oh yeah, it's night marchers, but don't worry. They're my 'ohana."

Receiving no reply from Glen, the man turned around to see Glen running across the street with his arms in the air, waving back and forth. He ran to the beach and quickly buried the burning fire, enlisting the help of a few students and then ushered everyone back onto the bus with a mad urgency. Glen was so terrified by what might happen that all he could think of was leaving immediately. In the process of doing that, he almost left his Hawaiian friend behind!

☾

In her book, "The Night Marchers," Helen Hoyt tells another story about a man from Wai'anae who said he witnessed the night marchers twice in his life.

The first incident happened on a still night when the only sound they could hear was pounding surf nearby. Suddenly, above the sound of the crashing waves, the man, his wife, and their friend heard the unmistakable sound of the pahu and the nose flute. He dared to look out the window and said he could see the marchers of the night partially hidden by swirling mists. Suddenly, they were gone, and the only sound left was the churning sea. The following day, his friend explained that the man's grandson had died, and his ancestors came with the 'oi'o to welcome him to the afterlife. Nearly a month after that night, a letter came informing the couple that their grandson had died in a battle in Europe on the same night they witnessed the ghost army marching outside their home.

The second time the man witnessed the 'oi'o was years later, as the ghostly army made their way past the man's home. At the end of the procession was his great-granddaughter's love, bloody and battered, still wearing his military uniform. He was killed in the war before the young couple could be officially married.

'Ewa Plains

'Ewa has long been known as the Plains of Kaupe'a. It is the realm of the ao kuewa, the realm of the wandering spirits of people who were not found by their family 'aumākua upon their death, or had not earned their rightful place among them, or had not found the leina a ka 'uhane to leap into Pō. The spirits wander the wiliwili grove, feeding on pulelehua (moths) and nananana (spiders) while hoping to find someone who could save them and carry them into the netherworld.

I was called to the relatively new community of Ocean Pointe in 2005 by a family that believed night marchers were assaulting them during certain times of the month. The children claimed that the beds they slept in would move and shake while they were still in them. The wife claimed to smell the horrible stench of something foul. The husband, a newly retired military veteran, was the last person in the household to be convinced of his family's claims.

Suffering from terrifying nightmares since his most recent deployment, he dreamed that his team was calling out in anguish and pain, begging him to come and help them. He suddenly awoke in a pool of sweat, but the calling from his dream did not end. He heard it in his backyard. Looking down from his second-story bedroom window and into the yard, he saw them. An entire cadre of Hawaiian chiefs and warriors calling out his name in unison, "Kamanawa."

By the time he ran downstairs and opened the back door to the yard, the chiefs and warriors were gone. Strangely, the contents of his storage locker were strewn about everywhere, even though the storage locker was still locked, and he had the only key.

My first suggestion was to grow ti plants along the side and front of the house, but the husband wasn't sure the Homeowner's Association would allow it. He said he'd ask for approval, and I told them that the only other bit of advice I had was that if there was indeed a night marchers' path coming through his home, they should perhaps move his storage locker and then rearrange his bedroom and those of his children. I explained that the night marchers were here long before us, and instead of attempting to cleanse or bless the home to be rid of them, it would be easier to come to an understanding and adjust.

"They have to adjust?" the husband asked curiously.

"No, you have to adjust. That is why you must rearrange the furniture in your rooms. You should be fine after that."

All these years later, all is still well with that home in Ocean Pointe.

Processions of the 'oi'o have been seen or heard in Hono'uli'uli, Ka Makana Ali'i Mall, Barbers Point, Ocean Pointe, Pu'uloa, and One'ula.

Waikele

Our history tells us that the Waikele area was the site of an annual Makahiki procession and also a place where warriors trained their bodies and minds during that time of peace. When the former K-Mart opened many years ago, stories began to surface about spirits haunting the stock room and that once, the entirety of the store was found in shambles when employees would come to work in the morning.

The overnight stock team was responsible for filling the shelves when no customers were in the building. The late hour allows them to work quickly and uninterrupted to have the merchandise neatly presented upon store opening. It was the mid-1990s when the Kmart store in Waikele was newly built. A friend who worked in overnight stock shared his story with me.

It was only a little after midnight, and the teams were in their groove when the electronics started going crazy. The lights in the store became painfully bright and then slowly went dark and then turned bright again. My friend said this went on for a few minutes until the lights went back to their normal brightness. As it was just in time for their first break, most of the employees retreated to the break room.

Suddenly, he heard a loud scraping sound to his left, and when he looked in that direction, he could just see the end of one of the shelves moving toward his direction. Other team members were running towards him, screaming, trying to get out of the way of the long shelves that were moving fast across the floor. They said no one was pushing them.

Before everyone finally made it out of the emergency exits, employees said the store was filled with the smell of sulfur and the deafening sound of drums. No one wanted to re-enter the store until the manager arrived with the morning crew. Daylight revealed that all the shelves were shoved to one side of the building as if a giant hand swept them aside.

☾

I learned of one of the more recent tales of the Waikele area on one of my ghost tours. The young woman explained that she and some friends were hanging out in the parking lot late at night when they witnessed a line of floating lights coming through the Kmart building. The lights got brighter as they entered the parking lot and then disappeared as they approached the chain-link fence. There were no apparitions carrying torches or sounds of drums or marching feet, but fourteen people saw little balls of flames following one another in a long line.

Moanalua

The Maui chief, Kalaikoa, once lived at Moanalua. He built a long house, named it Kauwalua, and had it filled with the bones of his enemies. The bones were stripped and bound together, and the skull was set upon each bundle. The bundles were then placed inside and all around the hale so that, when seen from a distance, it looked like a company of living men. Kalaikoa's hale iwi stood at Lapakea on the slope into Moanalua on the upper side of the old road.

In 1972, Hawaii's Living Treasure, Rubellite Johnson, described a tale of night marchers for a newspaper editorial. In it, she says that Rudolph Tai, a patriarch of the Mormon Church in Hawai'i, used to live in the old Damon Tract housing before it was demolished. One night, at midnight, he heard the sound of the ghost army approaching from the uppermost part of Moanalua Valley. As the procession moved closer, he could hear their chants and the hiss of their burning torches as the night marchers made their way toward the sea.

The sounds became louder and louder until Rudolph Tai could stand it no more and had to hold his hands to his ears to keep the noise out. Then, after two long hours, the chants and the marching slowly faded away.

But, happening at the same time...

The late watchman on a small ship anchored in Pearl Harbor recorded a most curious site in his log. From midnight until 2 a.m., the man saw a string of torches moving slowly from the top of Moanalua Valley, winding toward the sea, where they disappeared.

☾

In 1986, I took part in a video filmed at the Leeward Community College media center. It was a scene from a David Mammet play called "Sexual Perversity In Chicago." The director of the video, Mara, was a lot of fun and full of enthusiasm. After the video was cut and edited, all the actors and the media people were invited to Mara's house to watch the completed project.

Mara lived in the Red Hill military housing right up the road from Moanalua Kaiser hospital. We all enjoyed the pupus and had a great time seeing ourselves on video. Everyone hung out afterward for more food and drinks and interesting conversation.

Inside Mara's house was a black burn mark along the top of the wall, a little below the ceiling. It extended from one end of her living room to the other. When I had a chance, I pulled her aside and asked her about it.

"That's from the night marchers. They come right through my house and the other houses next to mine. They march straight out to Aliamanu crater. Until I put up potted ti leaf plants in my living room, it was worse! The whole place was scorched. Good thing my aunty is a kahuna. She's the one who told me what to do; otherwise, this place would have burned down!" Mara excused herself after her matter-of-fact explanation and returned to her hostess duties.

☾

Researchers and retired staff of Moanalua High School have said that the campus lies near the site of an old heiau that was destroyed long ago. The school is allegedly in the path of the huakaʻi pō.

Downtown Honolulu

In terms of cities, Honolulu may resemble any other with its high rises and traffic grid. Busy during the day but fairly quiet at night, the city's ghosts are ever-present.

Several years ago, a group of attorneys on the 23rd floor of a building in the heart of Downtown Honolulu called me. They believed that their security cameras captured the night marchers on video.

A Hawaiian woman from the cleaning staff was working one night when a column of mist appeared. She reportedly died the next day, but the following month, a security guard claimed to have seen the ghost of the same woman in line with the night marchers, walking through the office corridor right through the wall where they disappeared. They said I was not allowed to actually view the video for security reasons, but the guard and the office staff were thoroughly frightened by what they'd witnessed.

It is said that the night marchers make their way down from Pu'u o Waiho Ana. Abbreviated to Puowaina, the "hill of offering or sacrifice" is more commonly known today as Punchbowl Crater. From this hill of sacrifice, the night marchers are said to travel straight through the busy city along Bishop Street.

Kaimukī

In days long past, Hawaiians used to cook the root of the kī (ti) plant. The result was a caramelized confection that Isabella Aiona Abbott said tastes like molasses. The neighborhood just above Waikiki is known as Ka-imu-kī, the ti oven, because menehune cooked kī in the underground ovens here.

Pu'u 'o Kaimukī is a hill that sits next to the local fire station. There is a procession that begins there and makes its way down to Esther Street towards a quiet school near the Honolulu Zoo. One can hear a succession of barking dogs, giving a hint as to where and when the marchers are traveling. Once it reaches the school, the 'oi'o disappears and then reappears near Kaimana Beach. Witnesses have said that this procession is made up of only wahine, and they march on the night of Hua. I don't have a great deal of information on this march, but because it's a wahine procession, perhaps it's not meant for me, as a man, to know.

Kapiʻolani Park

In 1877, King Kalakaua dedicated 200 acres of Royal Land for use as a public space and created what is now the second oldest public park on Oʻahu. Named after his wife, Queen Kapiʻolani, and located at the base of Diamond Head, the expansive park is a place for all kinds of gatherings, parties, and sports events.

The park sits just below the site of Papaʻenaʻena heiau. It was built as a luakini heiau dedicated to Kū and was the beginning and ending point of many ceremonial processions. These marches were often solemn, and strict kapu were enforced. They passed through the area now known as Kapiʻolani Park on sacred nights and reportedly still do today.

Many old veterans of the Honolulu Police Department have shared their late-night otherworldly encounters in Kapiʻolani Park. One officer remembers receiving a notice from dispatch regarding a disturbance in the park. Upon arriving on his Cushman cart near the bandstand, he heard high shrill screams. He started his vehicle and followed the sound.

He said that the screams were coming from the fenced-off area in the park near the Waikiki Shell, where he saw a local woman being dragged across the grass by her feet. What pulled her along was a group of men that looked like Hawaiian warriors. Some were carrying torches, but the rest seemed to be crowding around the poor, screaming woman. The thing was, he could see right through them like they were ghosts. They were beating her with what looked like clubs while others appeared to be stabbing her with spears. He immediately called for backup while at the same time drove towards the mob.

The officer said that, as he got closer, some invisible force flipped his Cushman upside down, and he went tumbling out and hit the ground hard. He lost consciousness after that.

When he came around, other officers were gathered around him, but the mob of ghostly warriors was gone. However, on the grass lay a badly beaten homeless woman.

"Imagine having to fill out that report?" He chuckled.

"Did you?" I asked.

"Psshh, no! I mean, I filled out a report but not exactly like I witnessed. You understand, right?"

☾

In her 1937 book, "Hawaiian Tapestry," Antoinette Withington writes about her interview with a man named George, who lived in Waikiki at the time. He pointed to the area of the old heiau and said that the nightly procession used to march through Waikiki and end up there at the heiau. By the description, the site to which he referred must have been Papaʻenaʻena.

George said he saw the procession once when he was walking home alone, just as it began to get dark. Ahead of him, he saw a strange cloud of dust, but it shone silver. He looked up at the moon and realized that it was just a sliver of a new moon, so he knew it wasn't the moon that caused this dusty cloud to shine.

As George looked on, he began to see figures of people, and he knew it must be the procession. He crouched down beside a boulder so the figures could not see him, and he watched. He described old people and young people, they walked towards the old heiau, and then he heard the drums beating. He tried to see if his young cousin, who had died a year before, was present, but she was not in the procession.

Withington states that she learned that old George was once an interpreter in King Kalakaua's court in his younger days, and his experience and opinions were held in the greatest respect by all who knew him.

In another account, a visitor, who had never heard of the procession of spirits, explained to Withington an inexplicable event that occurred. From her hotel, on two separate occasions, she saw moving lights upon the water. The first night, she saw only the lights moving about, but the second night, the lights seemed to leave the water. It was then that the woman saw that they were figures, like people, each one carrying a light. In a procession, the strange figures walked along the beach and on towards Diamond Head.

Nuʻuanu

Nuʻuanu is perhaps most famous for its association with Kaleleakeʻanae, the famous battle between Kalanikupule's 9,000 warriors and Kamehameha's invading army of 12,000 warriors from Hawaiʻi.

Kalanikupule's army, already weakened from the Battle of Aiea and a failed attempt to seize two well-armed merchant vessels, was outnumbered and outgunned. Anticipating Kamehameha's attack, he stationed his chiefs at strategic points throughout the Nu'uanu Valley.

The landing of Kamehameha's forces along the beaches from Waikiki to Wai'alae was unopposed by the commoners they encountered, and the Hawai'i warriors took four days to gather food and scout out enemy positions. The first battle clashed near Punchbowl crater and moved upland from there.

The final spot, the Nu'uanu Pali, was the end of the grueling 6-mile battle. The O'ahu forces were defeated, either by jumping off the precipice or by hand-to-hand combat. It was desirable to be killed in battle, for then your mana would be preserved for your bloodline. It was better than being captured and turned into a slave or becoming a sacrifice and having your bones made into tools like fishhooks.

Many O'ahu warriors were able to escape over into Kalihi and the Windward side, including Kalanikupule, but there were hundreds of soldiers who fought for hours and hours to the very end in order to help their ali'i and their comrades escape.

The late Mayor John H. Wilson, who built the first road over the Pali in his youth, told about visiting the area on a surveying trip and finding more than 800 skulls, together with other human bones, littering the ground beneath the cliff. Many skulls were collected and sold to museums, while it is said that the rest were left where they were. The skeletons were buried by the dirt and rock that came from constructing the road.

Many people claim to have seen warriors late at night at the Pali. Tall, muscular men dressed in malo, holding spears or leiomano, the shark tooth weapon. Other witnesses have claimed to see spirits marching in procession at the Pali and through the valley below. From the Pali, along the ridge, passing through Kaniakapupu to Puiwa, through Mauna'ala, and down through lower Nu'uanu valley, walk the sleepless specters of Hawaii's huaka'i o ka pō.

☽

The procession of Menehune is also said to make its way from Hawai'i Island, stopping at a place on each island as they make their way to Kaua'i. When they reach O'ahu, it is said that the menehune climb to the peak at Pu'ulanihuli before coming down the ridge to the Pali area, where they have their meal before traveling on to their home in Wainiha on Manokalanipo, also known as Kaua'i. The procession travels in a single line in the dark of night, making their way to their resting spot before the sun comes up.

Kāne'ohe

In 1929, Harold K.L. Castle built his grand mansion on a 20-acre estate at the base of the Pali. Five hundred feet above sea level, the estate had a steep cliff face jutting up to one side and sweeping views of the Windward coast on the other. When it was built, the Pali highway hadn't yet been made, and a narrow road wound its way through a thick forest of bamboo and banyan trees. That little road crossed over Kahana'iki stream before opening to a wide courtyard exposing a grand home that seemed to be magically suspended from the slopes of the Pali. The 25-room mansion, its supplementary buildings, garages, kennels, and mountain road were built at the cost of about $300,000.

Known as Paliku, the home entertained such celebrities as Spanish nobility, war heroes, and Hollywood film stars.

But after only 17 years, in June of 1946, the Castle family sold the estate to the Roman Catholic Church for only $200,000. The estate then became St. Stephen's Seminary. Part of the building, with its mirrors and Venetian candlesticks, became the seminary's chapel. The private library became the main classroom. And one wing of the top floor was screened in and became the dormitory where the teenage seminarians and their teachers slept.

One October night in 1946, the boys were sleeping in their beds when a sound could be heard from high up on the hill. Each seminarian had a bed, a chair, and on top of the chair, a stainless steel washbowl about 4-5 inches deep. The dorm looked out at the Pali slopes that stretched high above them. One priest described the sound as a tapping. Another thought it sounded more like a methodical clicking. It came closer and closer, edging down the mountain like a swollen river.

Father Cullinen listened as whatever was causing the tapping came closer and closer, making its way down the mountain. Suddenly, the tapping sound entered the room, and the washbowls seemed to come alive, rattling faster and faster. Then the tapping went back up the mountain. Father Cullinen watched as this happened several times that night. The clamor was so loud that it woke the young men from their slumber, all except one. This one young man slept through the entire racket, but he was not left undisturbed as his neck started to swell to the size of a grapefruit. Unsure of what else to do, Father

Cullinen placed a crucifix next to the sleeping boy's neck, and the swelling subsided.

The presence, they said, that was responsible for the racket came to a stop at the sleeping boy's bed. The priests watched in horror as the boy's body was pushed deep into the bed, then brought back up, over and over again. He didn't levitate or actually leave the bed. Although there was no person or visible entity there, it was as if the boy was pressed deep down into the bed by a strong man, then released. Finally, without warning, it left the boy alone. But whatever it was, it wasn't gone.

From the dormitory, there was a spiral staircase that led to a huge kitchen. Soon, the group could hear the sound of dishes and pots and pans being thrown around. When the noise stopped, Father Cullinen went down to investigate and found the kitchen items strewn all over.

Because of this incident, the seminary was closed, and the priests were requested not to discuss what they witnessed. Only years later were they able to finally describe what happened.

In 1961, Retired Bishop of Honolulu, Joseph Ferrario, said he understood a blessing was done, but it probably wasn't an exorcism. The boy, who slept through what has now been termed a "diabolical obsession," never returned.

Now, this isn't just a ghost story that has been passed along. Whatever happened at the seminary, according to Ferrario, happened. There is no question about that.

"It was real," he said, "Told and corroborated by prominent men in the Roman Catholic Church."

While the church deems the incident a "diabolical obsession," to a Hawaiian, the description brings to mind the night marchers making their way down the Pali, through the seminary building, and across the property.

Kailua

Described as the former residence of many of O'ahu's ruling chiefs, Kailua is also home to Hauwahine, the mo'o. She guards Kawainui and shares the pond's wealth with the people of the village but also punishes those who are greedy. However, that is a story for another time.

When he was a boy, long before Kawainui became a wildlife refuge and protected area, Randall and a bunch of his friends hiked out to the marsh to go fishing. It was already very late in the afternoon, but the boys had no care about the time. There was a secret spot in the marsh in which they were always lucky to catch lots of fish, and once they reached that spot, they each quickly began whipping with their fishing poles.

They hadn't been there for much more than a few minutes when they suddenly heard the sound of beating drums. Looking around for the source of the pounding cadence, they saw torch lights moving through the trees.

Randall said that he doesn't recall if they abandoned their fishing poles or not. What he does remember is that while coming up the trail to the marsh, it was an easy walk, there was nothing on the path. However, while running back down the same way to escape the ghostly night marchers, they found the path blocked by a huge boulder. After much effort, they were able to make their way around the giant rock and get back to the road where they'd left their bicycles. He and his friends mounted their bikes and rode as hard as they could.

"It's over forty years later, and I've never gone back there," Randall said, "It's still too scary after all these years."

Punalu'u

Keali'imaika'i, younger brother of Kamehameha I, had a son named Kekuaokalani. It was prophesied that Kekuaokalani would be the next great ruler after Kamehameha. In those ancient days, when the young ali'i was born, his upbringing was taken charge by Kahonu, the priest, and his wife, both of whom were iwikuamo'o, close relatives of the ali'i.

When the young ali'i was a month old, the council of chiefs approved the request of Kahonu to segregate their royal charge to a different island. In his capacity as priest, Kahonu sought to maintain the dignity and sacredness of his royal charge, for he was of the kapu moe status, the highest rank of ali'i when a commoner was sure to be killed if even his shadow fell upon the house of the ali'i. With the approval of the council, the group set off from Hawai'i Island to O'ahu.

When the voyagers arrived in Punalu'u, Kahonu and his wife took their young charge to the densest part of the forest in the deep solitude of the uplands of the mountains, a place called Kawaiakāne-Kawaiakanaloa, where the ali'i was nurtured. The other kāhuna and traveling companions were made by Kahonu to remain at Maliko to erect a house for his royal charge and to repair heiau Kaumaka'ula'ula.

The heiau became famous for wonderful and mysterious things. On the approach of the sacred nights of Kāne and Kanaloa, every six months, the eyes of all the pigs near the boundaries of the temple would turn red. Hence the name, Kaumaka'ula'ula, the appearance of red eyes. The place is spoken of as hidden, "he heiau huna ia," a most sacred temple. Sounds of the pahu (drum), the 'ohe hanu ihe (the nose flute), ipu hokiokio (the whistling gourd), and the voices of the kahuna chanting in prayer could be heard by anyone in the vicinity. It is said that this has continued from its founding up until the early 1900s.

Sadly, nothing remains of the heiau structure today. However, the sounds of the pahu, the 'ohe hanu ino, the ipu hokiokio, and the oli of the kahuna can still be heard on the nights of Kāne and Kanaloa.

Lā'ie

Far from the bustle of the city, the North Shore of O'ahu is not immune to sightings of the ghostly warriors. The inhabitants of a cottage located at the base of a heiau on the North Shore reported that Night marchers kept coming through their house. Their main complaint was the racket caused when the front and back doors would fly open. While they were unable to cause the warriors' path to change, they solved the problem of the noise by leaving the doors open.

☾

In his weekly newspaper column, Bob Krauss mentions a discussion he had with a woman while she was cutting his hair. She said that where she lived in Lā'ie was a Pu'uhonua, and Pō Kāne nights would bring the night marchers. On two occasions, she saw the torches on the water and could hear the sound of the pu and the pahu and the voices of people chanting.

Kahuku

When reviewing a map of the ahupua'a of O'ahu, one might notice that there are two strips of land near Kahuku Point that are labeled 'Oi'o. The name implies that these ahupua'a contained trails on which the night marchers traveled. Unlike the ahupua'a, Lā'iemalo'o and Lā'iewai that have retained their complete names, the differentiating names of the pair of ahupua'a called 'Oi'o have been lost.

During WWII, the Army built an airfield at Kahuku. The runways faced the sea, with the main barracks built upon a knoll in line with the runway. The rest of the barracks were constructed about the runways.

Among the Hawai'i recruits was a group of Nisei, second-generation Japanese-American citizens. Bunking in the main barracks, the Nisei soon requested to be moved into the smaller barracks off to one side of the runway.

When the captain asked why they were dissatisfied, they told him that they were experiencing odd disturbances at night. While some men said they were being choked in their sleep, others said they were having nightmares every night. Suggesting the men were suffering from indigestion, the captain dismissed their pleas.

Soon, the Hawai'i soldiers made friends with a group from the mainland and convinced them to swap living arrangements, to which the captain agreed. As the Nisei slept peacefully in the smaller barracks, the mainland soldiers soon began complaining to the captain about being choked in their sleep.

Finally, the captain inquired as to what might be causing problems. An old Hawaiian who had lived in the area stated that the airfield had been constructed right over the path of the night marchers as they traveled to an old heiau in the mountains.

When people think of Maui, the first things that come to mind are often Haleakalā, the Road to Hana, or its well-traveled, demigod namesake, Maui. However, Maui abounds with the rich history of its ali'i and akua. Kamehameha took Ka'ahumanu, who was born in Hana, as his wife and set up his kingdom in Lahaina, then known as Lele, thus cementing the bond and control of the island.

Honokohau Valley

As Ke'eaumoku lay dying, he warned Kamehameha that the one person he should fear was his daughter and Kamehameha's own wife, Ka'ahumanu, for should she ally herself with another man, that husband or lover would rise against Kamehameha. Based on this warning, Kamehameha placed a kapu upon his wife, Ka'ahumanu.

Despite the kapu, Ka'ahumanu seduced the handsome Kanihonui, and their affair was discovered. The fact that the young man was the 19-year-old son of Kamehameha's half-sister whom he raised and one of Kamehameha's favorites was not enough to save him. Kanihonui was promptly executed at Papa'ena'ena heiau on the slope of Diamond Head.

In Honokohau Valley, in West Maui, a procession of warriors led by the headless specter of Kanihonui is said to have been seen, reportedly leaving several men dead in its path.

'Īao Valley

'Īao Valley itself is steeped in a kind of palpable atmospheric history. The crescendo of the Battle of Kepaniwai, Battle of the Dammed Waters of 'Īao, lay in the river itself that was dammed with the bodies of slain warriors. People often wonder about the ghostly appearances of Hawaiian warriors at 'Īao.

Due to some close personal connections, Mr. Dover was allowed to remain in the 'Īao Valley State Monument parking area after hours. There, he and his female companion explored several areas of the park, engaging in a forbidden couple's secret desires. As they finally returned to their rental car, they were suddenly blocked off by a long procession of phantom torches.

The pair saw that the procession appeared to be coming from the recesses of the valley. It then came up the hill toward them in a long line as it moved through the parking lot. A second procession continued along the path of the river itself. Dover noted that there was an eerie, unnerving silence that accompanied the whole incident. However, he said that he had no idea that he and his friend were about to suffer a spiritual after-shock.

He intimated to me that when the sound came, it was like the blast of hundreds of cannons being fired all at once, and it came at full volume; the deafening sound of drums, foot marches, chants, and wailing, pitiful mournful wailing that raised the hackles on his neck. And the stench of something long dead and rotted away, coupled with the reek of sulfur, made him throw up his drive-thru dinner.

Dover said his female companion stripped completely naked and lay flat on the parking lot blacktop. In a second, she pulled him down next to her and then covered him with her body. It felt like hours had passed, but when the whole incident was over, the woman got off him and jumped to her feet. The first rays of the early morning were coming up, and that's when he noticed his friend hurrying frantically to put her clothes on. He was horrified to see hand and footprint bruise marks all over her front and most of her back.

"Take me back to my car," she was breathing heavily now. "Get me out of here and take me back to my car right now."

On the way back to the rent-a-car dealer at the airport, Dover said that he tried to talk to his female companion, but she would not let him get in one word.

"Lucky thing I know how to chant my genealogy! These bruises are what I had to suffer because I was trying to protect you, but you know what? This ain't worth it. We're done. You better hope your wife never finds out about us because if she does and you or your wife ever bring this to my house? I will ruin you in a very public way, you understand?"

"I never saw her again after that," Dover shrugged his shoulders.

I finally noticed his full head of white hair, "You got a young-looking face for someone with white hair."

"I'm thirty-one," he sighed, "The white hair came after we saw the night marchers at 'Īao. My wife likes it. She said it makes me look distinguished."

"Did she ever find out about... you know?" I had to ask since his whole story is based on his affair.

"Knowing karma, she will. It will probably be during some unexpected moment, and all hell will break loose."

"I think she knows," I replied while looking up at him above my glasses.

"Oh yeah?" He answered arrogantly, "What makes you think so?"

"Your white hair. It doesn't matter what your explanation was when you told her how your hair turned white. It's the questions that she'll keep asking until she breaks you, and you finally end up telling her the truth."

Olowalu

If a person made the mistake of breaking a kapu in which his punishment was death, his only chance of survival was to reach a pu'uhonua, a place of refuge. Since a pu'uhonua protected the kapu breaker, no physical harm could come to him if he reached the boundaries of this place of refuge. The pu'uhonua also protected warriors who were defeated in battle and civilians during times of war. Olowalu was one such place. It was also one of the largest agricultural valleys in West Maui and is fronted by one of Hawaii's most unique reef systems.

However, Olowalu is sadly most famous for the massacre that happened there. In 1790, American Captain Simon Metcalf, in command of the ship the Eleanora, ordered the brutal murder of hundreds of Hawaiians in what was then called Kalolopahu, the spilled brains, thus dramatically changing the area for over two hundred years.

But the legends and the spirituality of the place remain. In Olowalu, there live moʻo beings, sightings of menehune continue, spirits linger, and the drums of the huakaʻi pō can still be heard on the Nights of Kāne.

Wailea

Although this area was once part of the Ulupalakua horse ranch, polo is not played here. The original name for Polo Beach is Keoneopolo, which is a reference to the sands of time and the night marchers.

Up in Kula, the rainy weather fills the rolling stream. Strange gusts of wind pass through Kaipoioi Gulch, carrying thick fog resembling wraiths. That Gulch and stream go down toward Keoneopolo, and on certain nights, the March of the Spirits is seen and heard as it travels westward to the sea.

MOLOKA'I

Traveling to the quiet island of Moloka'i is almost like going back in time. While residents of the island do enjoy modern conveniences, these things fail to drown out the peace and serenity and the sense of neighborly closeness. However, while the people of Moloka'i welcome visitors, they refuse to be trampled on. Tradition says that when Pa'ao returned from Tahiti with his warriors to invade Moloka'i, they found the people waiting for them in silence. Standing together, the people began to 'oli, softly at first and kept chanting until the sound became like a roar. The warriors' spears were useless as they kept falling short of their intended targets. Those who attempted to attack fell back into the water, choking. Just as Moloka'i was not conquered that day, the practice of pule o'o was used several times in the following centuries hence the name, O Moloka'i i ka pule o'o (Moloka'i of the powerful prayer), as it is said that outside chiefs have never conquered the island.

Kalama'ula

In 1921, the U.S. Congress enacted The Hawaiian Homes Commission Act as a homesteading program to place native Hawaiians (defined in the Act as those of 50 percent or more

Hawaiian blood) on designated lands in Hawai'i. The first Hawaiian homestead community built after the establishment of the Act was Kalama'ula. The land was full of kiawe trees and had no running water, but the men, women, and children who were chosen to live there worked hard to build their homes and make a life for themselves.

There is a tale about the 'oi'o making their way through the old commission house on the Kalama'ula Homestead. Despite warnings from the locals, the commission house was built on top of the old heiau. One night, around midnight, the people in the house stated that they were awakened by voices chanting behind the house, accompanied by the sound of the ukeke and pahu. The noise lasted nearly an hour before it began to make its way toward the house, through the front door, and out the back before fading off. In the morning, their neighbor explained that the procession comes through the heiau every year around that time.

Kawela

Before Kamehameha was king, Kapi'ioho'okalani, an ali'i of O'ahu, attempted to overtake Moloka'i. Most of the chiefs of Moloka'i were descended from Hawai'i Island, so Alapa'i, the ruling chief of Hawai'i Island at the time, came to the defense of the tiny island. The forces of Hawai'i joined with those of Moloka'i in a formidable alliance, and the fighting went on for four days, with neither army gaining much ground over the other.

On the fifth day, every able-bodied man joined the fight. The armies met at Kawela, and the battle raged from early morning until the afternoon. The Moloka'i forces attacked from the hills, and those of Hawai'i attacked from the direction of the sea. The O'ahu forces were surrounded and hemmed into a small space where Kapi'ioho'okalani, along with many of his chiefs and warriors, was slaughtered.

Residents in the area say that the ghostly armies still march through Kawela on their way to battle.

Mapulehu

'Ili'ili'opae is the largest heiau on Moloka'i and is estimated to have been built around the 13th century. Legend says that the menehune built Ili'ili'opae with the stones being brought from Wailau over ten miles away. In building this heiau, the Menehune stood side-by-side, passing each rock to the next person so that the stones never touched the ground. The heiau was completed in a single night, for which the Menehune each received a single opae (shrimp) as food.

'Ili'ili'opae was a powerful training center for kahuna. While we know there are many different types of kahuna, with the level of kahuna meaning master of his particular craft, as a luakini heiau, 'Ili'ili'opae saw hundreds of sacrifices. After their learning was complete, the kahuna educated at 'Ili'ili'opae were sent to work at other heiau.

During the season of Kāne, the men were summoned to the heiau by the beating of drums and loud shouting while women remained out of sight. As with most ceremonies for the gods, the process of sacrifice demanded that strict protocol be followed. Any infraction of the kapu meant certain death.

'Ili'ili'opae is nearly thirty miles away from the central town of Kaunakakai. My dear friend, Kahu Dave Wallace, said, "I am not familiar with night marchers going through Kaunakakai town but am very aware of the night marchers and spirits in and around 'Ili'ili'opae."

The area where the heiau, 'Ili'ili'opae, is built is called Mapulehu. West of the heiau, near the base of the ridge, stood Mapulehu Dairy.

"When the cows were brought over for the dairy, the cows went dry and would not give milk. Something was scaring them," explained Kahu Dave.

Pu'unānā

Because it is the highest point in West Moloka'i, Pu'unānā was a vital lookout point for ancient Hawaiians. At the height of nearly 1,400 feet, the view from atop Pu'unānā looks across the channel to Maui and Lāna'i, and on a clear day, one can even see Hawai'i Island.

It is said that, even though the native plants and trees are gone, and the land is dry, the processions of the huaka'i pō continue on certain nights.

Ho'olehua

Near the local airport and just a few miles away from the Kalaupapa lookout lies a small neighborhood called Ho'olehua.

Kahu Dave explains, "The night marchers that came through our homestead in Ho'olehua were athletes going to the Na'iwa Makahiki grounds located to the northwest of our homestead. We could see them carrying their spears and supplies, holua sleds, food."

Our friend, Anela, also describes night marcher encounters at their home in Ho'olehua when she was a child.

"When I first moved there, I didn't know why the chickens and all sounds would stop - literally ALL sound would cease - at around 3:00 AM at certain times of the month. You could hear the faint sounds of footsteps in the distance before they got closer, and they would always stop right at my bedroom window. That window was on the same wall as our front door."

She explains, "When we moved into that house, the front and back doors were in line with one another. Before settling into the house and having it blessed, my dad offset the front door so they were no longer in line with each other. As soon as the footsteps would stop, all the noises, all the nature sounds, would start up again."

☽ ○ ☾

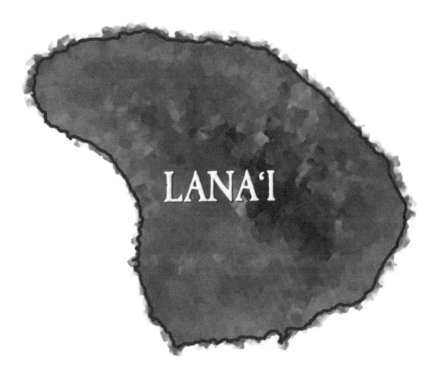

The fertile island of Lāna'i was once occupied by ghosts, and they were ruled by Pahulu, the ghost king of nightmares. After being exiled to Lāna'i for his mischievous deeds, Kaulula'au outsmarted Pahulu and his ghosts, finally destroying them all and making the island habitable by man. Today, the small, sparsely populated island boasts one school for all grades, one hospital and health center, and no traffic lights.

Lāna'i City

In the center of the island lies Lāna'i City. Our friend James Ishizaki described the town he grew up in as having little for teenagers to do. It is a close community, and the area is quiet… and haunted.

James explains that a night marcher's trail comes down from the mountains in the East toward the Social Hall. Dole Pineapple originally built the large bungalow-style home as the plantation manager's residence. The old house became a community center in the mid-1930s and was given the simple name "Social Hall."

James explains that his friend's mother used to live nearby and often heard the drums of the phantom army. From the Social Hall, the trail makes its way toward Hotel Lāna'i, through Dole Park and the nearby neighborhood, and finally makes its way toward The Lodge and the cemetery beyond. It was at this cemetery where James' friend got mysterious scratches on her back while exploring one night.

Kaiolohia

On the north shore of Lāna'i is a place called Kaiolohia, also known as "Shipwreck Beach." Aptly named, the first thing most people notice is the rusted hull of a WWII-era self-propelled fuel tanker. This shallow, rocky channel became a ship graveyard where dozens of ships were intentionally beached when their usefulness had expired.

Aside from beach combing and exploring, this area has a reputation for night marchers that gather beneath the Keawe trees on Pō Kāne.

☽ ○ ☾

Mokuokeawe, the Island of the Chief Keawe, is the largest island in our archipelago. Often referred to as the "Big Island," Hawai'i Island is also the birthplace of King Kamehameha I and the current home of Pele. There are not many places in the world where you can throw a snowball, hike through a tropical rainforest, and splash in the warm ocean all in the same day.

Hilo

It is estimated that the first inhabitants of Hilo arrived around 1100 AD. A quiet bay, fertile lands, and abundant fresh water made the place ideal for settling in and building a new life. Today, as the largest city on the island, Hilo serves as the official seat of the County of Hawai'i.

There are several hotels along the water's edge of Banyan Drive in Hilo. These hotels see numerous guests nightly, including residents who want to indulge in a staycation once in a while. However, there is one group of visitors who turn up at a particular hotel during a specific moon phase without a reservation. From the building's mauka side, they walk through the wall and the hotel rooms, exiting through the wall at the opposite end of the building on their way to the ocean. Lights dim and flicker, pictures on the wall shake or fall to the floor, and sometimes the furniture moves. The employees at the hotel know to make themselves scarce during that time. So far, there haven't been any reported deaths during one of these events. Not that anyone has admitted to anyway.

Kukuihaele

Pukui translates Kukuihaele as traveling light or torch, indicating that the legendary night marchers made their way through the area.

A man in his forties described what he thought of as an encounter with the phantom army. All he could say was that he was going to go fishing but just sat on his tailgate for a while, talking story with his friends. They heard drums, and one friend swore he heard the sound of the pū, the conch shell. The group wasted no time wondering if they were right or not; they jumped in their vehicles and left.

"We never fish at all that night. We just drove to my friend's house and drank beer, and played ukulele in his driveway. Fishing is supposed to be good during the full moon, but I don't think we're gonna go back there when the moon is full anymore."

Waipi'o

Lush, green Waipi'o Valley was a place perfectly fit for Hawaii's ruling class. Home to ali'i, the center of political discourse, the site of many important heiau, and also the site of Pa'akalana, one of the island's major pu'uhonua or places of refuge. The steep valley walls hold the burial caves of Hawaii's ancient kings. Waipi'o was also Kamehameha's childhood home. In this sacred place, the wide valley not only provided sustenance, but the mana held within its embrace offered protection from outside harm. It was there, in Waipi'o, that Kamehameha was proclaimed the future ruler of the islands.

Rev. Lyons, via Joseph Emerson, shared the most famous tale about the ghost of King Kamehameha leading his ghostly army in 1883. Since then, it is said that the procession is seen once a year, marching in silence, keeping perfect step on their way to Lua o Milu in Waipi'o Valley.

Kohala

In the year 1758, there appeared a great light in the sky with feathers like a bird. The night was cold and rainy, and a woman named Keku'iapoiwa was in labor. Around the hale were numerous chiefs and guards intending to "pinch off the tip of the wauke shoot" as they waited for a prophecy to be fulfilled. In other words, they were waiting to kill the child who might grow up to challenge the ali'i, Alapa'inui. When Keku'iapoiwa sounded the final bearing down of pain, the child slipped down onto the waiting kapa. A stranger then lifted the thatch at the side of the hale, wrapped the infant in kapa, and stole him away. In 1758, Halley's comet streaked its way across the skies over Hawai'i. The stranger was Nae'ole, an ali'i of Kohala. The infant was Kamehameha I. The place is Kohala.

In a 1971 article, Napua Stevens Poire describes her encounter as a child during a visit to their family matriarch's home at Kohala. When their kupuna decided to visit other relatives, the children took that time to explore the areas deemed kapu by their great aunt. Skipping and racing down the dirt road looking for adventure, the children were cautious at first and then grew reckless as they thought there was nothing to be afraid of.

Suddenly, the young Napua said, "I was aware of wind howling through the trees," but there were no trees. She then heard heavy footsteps, pounding drums, and murmuring voices. Horrified to find that she was alone, she watched the distant figures of the other children disappearing in a cloud of dust. As she stood, frozen with fear, the drums became louder, the footsteps seemed as if they were right upon her, and the murmur of voices became loud chants. She was abruptly shoved off the path, and a name was whispered in her ear.

She ran home as fast as she could and told her kupuna what had happened. It was explained to her that the name whispered in her ear was that of their ancestor who had saved her from the terrible fate of death by the 'oi'o.

Kawaihae

Kāpoūkahi, a prophet from the island of Kaua'i, said that Kamehameha would conquer all the islands if he built a large heiau at the hill dedicated to the god, Kūkā'ilimoku. Kamehameha went to work immediately, and thousands of men camped out on the hills for nearly a year to build the structure. According to Kāpoūkahi, rigid guidelines would have to be followed in order to please Kū, the war god. One requirement was that the heiau must be constructed from water-worn lava rocks, and it is believed that those rocks came all the way from Pololū valley. The workers formed a human chain about twenty miles long and transported the rocks, hand over hand, with Kamehameha himself laboring alongside his people.

When the heiau was finished, Kamehameha invited his cousin Keōua to attend the dedication ceremony. When he arrived, Keōua was slain, and his body was carried to the heiau and offered as the principal sacrifice to Kū. The death of Keōua ended all opposition on the island of Hawai'i. The heiau called Pu'ukoholā indeed brought about Kamehameha's rule over all the Hawaiian Islands.

Although it was the last major heiau built in Hawai'i and was in use for only twenty-eight years, its powerful mana still remains. Witnesses who reside near the area, as well as those who were only visiting, claim to have seen the 'oi'o marching to and from the heiau on several occasions.

Waikoloa

Historic petroglyph fields and ancient fishponds seem to be overshadowed by two huge golf courses and a sprawling resort. Locals in the Waikoloa area say that when developers were building the Hilton Waikoloa Resort, a Kahuna advised them to leave a particular path bare and not build over it. Otherwise, they would regret it.

Nearby at Puakō, there are ki'i pohaku (petroglyphs) that depict long lines of human figures that are said to represent processions of men. One historian stated that his friend claimed to have seen the night marchers at Puakō.

Kailua-Kona

Kamehameha I initially made Kailua-Kona his capital after defeating the last of the rival ali'i. His residence at Kamakahonu, where he took his last breath, is on the same site as a modern hotel.

In a series of published oral history interviews with kūpuna and kama'aina, one kupuna talked about the huaka'i pō. As a youngster, the man said that his tūtū had a house that overlooked Kailua Bay. They used to see the lights of the huakaʻi pō coming from the small lighthouse behind the Ahuʻena Heiau at Kamakahonu, traveling along the edge of the bay on their way down to where Hale Hālawai is. The kupuna said that his elders used to watch from a distance but didn't want the children to watch and tried to make them stay in the room.

☾

Also in Kona, Kepelino describes an encounter that a man shared with him.

Just after nightfall, the young man was on his way home when he saw a long line of marchers in the distance coming toward him. Afraid to be seen, he climbed over a stone wall and sat very still. He could see that the warriors were about seven feet tall. The procession comprised both men and women, and they walked four abreast while their feet didn't even touch the ground. One of the warriors stepped out of the line and crouched alongside the wall where the man was hiding. As each file passed, he heard voices call out, "Strike!" and his protector answered, "No! No, he is mine!" The young man continued to watch as the procession passed and his protector rejoined the march.

A month later, the man was again returning home late at night. As he drew closer to the spot where he saw the ghostly warriors before, he heard the sound of the ipu and chanting. The man came close enough to see many of the men and women he had seen in the previous procession; however, they were not marching this time. The women danced the ʻalaʻapapa, a type of ancient hula, and the men were involved in mokomoko (wrestling) and other games of the past. All the while, there was chanting and drumming.

As he sat watching, the man heard someone call out, "There is the grandson of Kekuanoi!"

"Nevermind! We do not mind him!" said another.

Kekuanoi was the name of the man's grandfather, and he realized he was being discussed. He sat watching for a couple of hours and then went home. But before he shared what happened, his grandfather said he had seen it all.

He said, "I know that you have been with our people of the night; I saw you sitting by watching the sports."

In the old days, these marches and events were common in the Ka'u district. They used to march and play games practically on the same ground as in life.

Kona Hema (South Kona)

In ancient times, Kona Hema had the largest population of people. With rich, volcanic soil, consistent rain, and pristine ocean waters, the area flourished in agriculture and fishing. Full of great historical significance, important heiau, battle sites, and burial grounds can be found within the Kona Hema borders. Also in South Kona sits Hōnaunau, home of one of the largest archaeological sites in Hawai'i, Pu'uhonua o Hōnaunau. This ancient and sacred place has been beautifully restored and is now part of the U.S. National Park Service, where visitors can learn more about ancient Hawaiian culture and customs.

In the 1980s, on a seemingly quiet evening, a woman had just started her evening bath when her two sons complained about hearing loud drums. At first, she brushed it off and ordered the children back to bed, but they insisted, explaining that the drum sounds were getting closer, coming down the trail from Hōnaunau. This got her attention, and she immediately thought of the night marchers.

She pulled on a mu'umu'u and ran into the boys' room, where she could hear the pounding of drums. Looking out the window, she could see a trail of yellow lights. With her husband gone, she called a neighbor who told her to turn off her lights, hide with her children, and not look under any circumstances. A friend who was a policeman called to see what was happening and, after her explanation, refused to come to check on them. The woman hid under the covers on the bed with her sons as the drums grew louder and seemed quite close. She had to look.

Peeking out the window, the woman could see that the torch lights stopped almost in front of her house, and then, for some reason, they turned around.

The family survived the night and the night marchers. However, there was a victim. The next morning, the woman's policeman friend came to check up on the family and told her that they found the body of an old Hawaiian man who liked to fish at night. There were no marks upon his body. They believe he had died of fright.

((

In another South Kona incident, a cultural practitioner describes a night when her uncle had his own encounter with the frightening procession. Drinking the day away, the uncle decided to walk the trail that, in the past, was meant for only ali'i. Suddenly, the report says, the uncle felt the presence of the night marchers and fell to the ground in fear. The chanting and drumming grew louder, along with the sound of weapons banging together and voices arguing in the darkness.

The uncle recalled hearing the spirit of a Hawaiian warrior telling him that he had no right to be there and he would be punished. Yet, another spirit said he was a descendant, and the 'oi'o agreed not to kill him.

The man showed up at his home battered from head to toe and visibly shaken. Most of his family doubted him but one. The storyteller explained that she'd seen her uncle drunk and seen him after a fight, but she had never seen him as terrified as he was that morning.

Maunakea

The tallest mountain in the Hawaiian Chain, Maunakea is a deeply sacred place to Hawaiians.

Named in Hawaiian creation chants, Maunakea was the first-born child of Papa and Wakea. Also known as Ka Mauna a Wakea, the Mountain of Wakea, it is considered to be kupuna and is held in high esteem. Ancient burials and ahu are found all over the face of the mauna. For ages, the summit of Maunakea was considered kapu and was only accessible to the highest chiefs or kahuna.

A Hawai'i Island park ranger and kupuna stated in a 2010 Environmental Impact Statement that the night marchers are constantly at work on the summit. He's had many visitors and employees that have had spiritual experiences and unexplained happenings because these guardians are always on duty. He recalled that he was escorting a Japanese film crew when the cameraman and the soundman noticed what looked like giants walking between two of the large telescopes. The ranger explained that these were the night marchers, the guardians of the mountain and the surrounding area.

Malama

In the Moku of Puna lies the ahupuaʻa of Malama. At the edge of Malama, along the bluffs, sits MacKenzie State Recreational Area. A well-known fishing site, the park was established in 1934 but was named in 1939 to honor Albert J. W. MacKenzie after his death. MacKenzie was a forest ranger who worked extensively in the Puna district, including planting nearly all of the ironwood trees in the park.

MacKenzie's daughter states that she camped in many places with her dad and remembers the ironwoods in the park being very small when she was still a little girl. She explained that many locals have said that the area was haunted by night marchers, but her father attributed the unusual sounds to waves crashing into the caves below the cliffs.

Locals say that they indeed hear the night marchers, especially while fishing there on the darkest nights.

Kalapana

At night, the darkness in Kalapana seems to envelop you in a cold embrace. In my mother's day, electricity in the area was unavailable in some places, and there were no street lights to mark your path, so on a moonless night, the darkness was nearly absolute.

It was late one night, and the family was walking home from a party at a nearby neighbor's house. Her siblings were all a bit drunk but being pregnant with me at the time, my mother was not. However, she suddenly became exhausted and decided to stop. Kneeling on the black sand, she dug a shallow hole, just big enough to accommodate her pregnant stomach, and took a minute to lay on her side to rest and enjoy the chilly, moonless night.

Suddenly, the air was filled with the sound of chattering voices exchanging excited gossip in Hawaiian. Without warning, the din of voices turned into chanting. My mother told me that she sat up and saw a large procession of people walking quickly, six abreast, as if they were in a hurry to get somewhere. Every man and woman in the parade held torches aloft, and the glow was a vibrant red color.

My mother began to call out in Hawaiian to ask the people where they were going as she thought they might be family and that she ought to join them. Her brother, Joe, suddenly appeared. He grabbed her from behind, forcing her down to the sand, holding on with one arm around her shoulder and the other hand covering her mouth. They stayed that way for several minutes.

Once Joe was sure the procession was gone, he admonished my mother for trying to join the procession of the gods, more particularly, the march of the goddess Hi'iaka, Pele's youngest and most favorite sister. The consequences of interrupting such a procession would have been severe.

Knowing where the ghostly night marchers travel is not merely enough to be able to avoid them. One should also know when to avoid these areas to ensure safe passage.

☽ ○ ☾

Chapter 4
Nānā i ka Mahina
Pay attention to the Moon

Since the time of the ancients, Hawaiian society was governed by a system in which religion was paramount. All aspects of political and social organization were affected. Within this 'Aikapu, this system of laws, it was understood that nothing occurred outside of the will of the gods. From planting crops to the birth of children to battles waged, 'oli and appeals were made to the akua. The kapu that were in place assured that the akua were acknowledged and respected to ensure success and prosperity.

The physical manifestation of the gods came in the form of kinolau, their spiritual embodiment. Every living being is a form of kinolau for the gods, as is the wind and rain, the clouds, the ocean current, and the movement of lava. Through their kinolau, Hawaiians recognized the akua and honored them.

The gods were close and ever-present and shared the earthly realm with the people who worshiped them. It was natural that every event, every occurrence was an occasion for prayer. The akua were there to guide, protect, and bless their worshipers but also to warn and punish them as necessary.

The Hawaiians of old, our kūpuna, were astute observers who were able to recognize and understand every aspect of the environment in which they lived. This knowledge was tied directly to the worship of the akua, and kapu were placed on ways that the people would go about their lives, ensuring that there would be enough sustenance for everyone.

The Kumulipo is just one example of their considerable powers of observation. The chant describes all the different flora and fauna both on land and in the sea around our island home. The keen observations of the Hawaiian people stretch towards the heavens as well, describing the movement of the stars and the many phases of the moon.

Following the helu pō, the phases of the moon over Hawai'i, was a common and vital part of life. Hawaiians were observant enough to understand that the helu pō affected the way plants grew, thus affecting the crop's success. The helu pō also had an effect on how tides and fish behaved and, in turn, affected the success of a fishing trip. Thus, the helu pō affected nearly every aspect of life, including farming and fishing, building hale and heiau, and conducting ceremonies. Aligning daily life with the cycles of Mahina, the moon, and constant prayers and offerings to the gods, helped to ensure success and abundance.

According to my mother, in our family's tradition, the phantom army marched on the last four phases of the moon, Kāne, Lono, Mauli, Muku. This knowledge has been passed down to her from her parents, who had learned it from their parents and so on, all the way back to time unrecorded. However, there are other traditions passed down in families of different areas, as well as traditions observed over time.

Although the many references we've come across and the many eyewitness accounts differ slightly, one thing they have in common is that encounters of the night marcher processions often coincide with certain phases of the moon. This seems to make sense since the most important ceremonies took place on certain kapu moon phases devoted to particular ceremonies and the worship of the gods. Following are moon phases said to be sacred for ceremonies.

▼▼▼

NA MAHINA KŪ

3 · Kūkahi   4 · Kūlua   5 · Kūkolu   6 · Kūpau

There are four nights specifically dedicated to Kū; Kūkahi, Kūlua, Kūkolu, and Kūpau. This was a time for physical activity. As Kū implies all things upright, these moons relate to standing, building, constructing, and creating structure. During Na Mahina Kū, on the 3rd through the 6th nights of the lunar cycle, one will observe Mahina slowly growing.

HUA

13 · Hua

This moon is sacred to Lono and is known to be a fertile night for many things. On this night, Mahina has a distinct egg shape. Sacred ceremonies for fertility, including that of the land and crops, occur during the 13th moon in Hua.

KŪ

Kū represents male power. He is the god of war and chiefs, the god of the forests, canoe making, and fishing. His elaborate heiau were of the luakini or po'okanaka class, and he demanded human sacrifices for important rituals. The mighty Kū is invoked through many different names when his assistance and blessings are requested.

A farmer will appeal to Kūkao'o, Kū of the digging stick, or to Kūkulia and Kūkeolowalu, Kū of dryland and wetland farming, for abundant crops. Fishermen worshiped Kū'ula or Kū'ulakai, Kū of the abundance of the sea, for a bountiful catch. In sorcery, a kahuna will pray to Kūwaha'ilo, Kū of the maggot-dropping mouth. Warriors will pray to Kūka'ilimoku, Kū the snatcher of land, Kūkeoloewa, Kū the supporter, and Kūho'one'enu'u, Kū pulling together the earth. Kūnuiakea, Kū of the great expanse, was the supreme one of all the Kū gods who lived in the highest heavens. There are many more Kū gods which people would worship for particular blessings or success.

According to Kū worship, any incident that might threaten the whole community may be absolved by building a heiau dedicated specifically to Kū; a war may be won, or a prolonged drought could be averted.

The ceremonies surrounding the building of a luakini heiau dedicated to Kū were strict and unforgiving. Death was dealt swiftly to anyone who was caught making the slightest mistake.

Like other gods, Kū takes many forms. His kinolau include the 'io, the hawk, the 'īlio, the dog, and the moa, the chicken. Plant forms of Kū include niu, the coconut, the 'ōhi'a tree, and 'ulu, breadfruit.

NA MAHINA PIHA

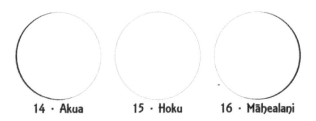

14 · Akua   15 · Hoku   16 · Māhealani

The nights of Akua and Māhealani, when the moon looks but is not completely full, and Hoku, the fullest moon, are the nights of Na Mahina Piha.

The moon, Akua, as its name implies, is the night of the gods. On Mahina's first night of fullness, the gods walk about the earth. Offerings are made on this kapu night seeking blessings to increase food and fish. This is the 14th moon.

Hoku, the fullest moon, as it applies to the Hawaiian calendar. It is favorable to plant anything on this 15th night as everything is animated by Mahina Hoku.

Māhealani, the 16th moon, was a sacred night when sacrifices were made.

He lā kapu heiau ia no kēia Pae ʻāina a puni, oia ka pō o Māhealani a ao ae.

It was a time of sacred ritual for this entire archipelago, the night of Māhealani, until the dawn of the next day.

(Nupepa Kuokoa, 6 April 1865)

LONO

The god of agriculture who created and controls the clouds and weather is Lono. He is also the god of peace and fertility. Heiau for Lono were constructed to pray for rain and abundant crops or relief from sickness. Offerings consisted of foods from the gardens and sometimes pua'a.

Lono is also the patron of the Makahiki. Each year, the annual event was announced by the kahuna upon the first observation of Makali'i over the eastern horizon at sunset. The timing of the Makahiki ceremonies and events were strictly tied to the moon phases of the season. During the Makahiki, kapu were placed on war, temple ceremonies, regular religious observances, and all work that was deemed unnecessary during the four-month period.

Along with several other god images, the Makahiki god was created at this time. The Makahiki god was a staff approximately ten feet long with an image carved at the top and a crosspiece tied to the staff's neck. Attached to the crosspiece were feather lei that fluttered about in the wind and white kapa, extending the full width of the cross piece that hung down longer than the pole. This Makahiki god was called Lonomakua.

Carried by men, Lonomakua traveled in procession to all the districts on the island to collect taxes in the form of foods, kapa, mats, and other goods. The collection assured the presenters a year of prosperity, sufficient rain, and bountiful crops. If the offerings were too little, the attendant chiefs ordered the ahupua'a to be plundered in the name of Lonomakua. When the god was deemed satisfied, he moved on to the next district.

Once the tax was paid, the rest of the four-month Makahiki period provided relief from the daily stresses of life under the kapu system. This was a time for hula and games of all sorts but particularly games of strength and skill. Pua'a the pig, humuhumunukunukuāpua'a the triggerfish, kukui, kalo, and 'uala the sweet potato are all kinolau of Lono.

NA MAHINA KALOA

24 · Kāloakūkahi   25 · Kāloakūlua   26 · Kāloapau

Kāloa is another term for Kanaloa and is affiliated with the ocean and such concepts. The period dedicated to the god Kanaloa is Na Mahina Kāloa, made up of the three moon phases, Kāloakūkahi, Kāloakūlua, and Kāloapau. Kāloa expresses broadness associated with the vast expanse of Moananuiakea. The waning moons of the 24th, 25th, and 26th nights show Mahina on her way to rest.

▼▼▼

NA MAHINA KĀNE

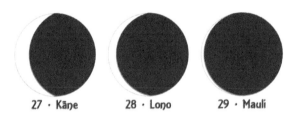

27 · Kāne   28 · Lono   29 · Mauli

Na Mahina Kāne, the three moons in the helu pō just before that last, darkest night are Kāne, Lono, and Mauli. Each of these nights are auspicious and foreboding for different reasons, and inspire reverence and humility. They are considered sacred to Kāne and reserved for the most sacred ceremonies.

Among these nights, however, Pō Kāne, the night of Kāne, is the time of greatest reverence. One will observe the slightest sliver of Mahina on this 27th night of the moon phase.

> He pō Kāne kēia, ke māʻau nei nā ʻeʻepa o ka pō.
>
> *This is the night of Kāne, for supernatural beings are wandering about in the dark.*
>
> Said of those who go wandering about at night.
> It is believed that on the night of Kāne, ghosts, demigods, and other beings wander about at will.
>
> (ʻŌlelo Noʻeau #908)

Lono, the 28th night is a highly auspicious time for sacred ceremonies. Mauli is the 29th moon phase. The night is set aside for spirits. On this night, one will see a mere slip of Mahina before she transitions to Muku.

MUKU

This is the night of the gods. This 30th night in the cycle is a transition moon when the cycle pauses, and Mahina remains unseen. A night for the gods to march, Muku is also considered a beginning or an ending, or both.

30 · Muku

KĀNE

The great Kāne is the "leading god among the great gods" and the creator of man. As Kānenuiakea, he is the creator of heaven, earth, and all things that dwell in each. He is the god of life and nature, freshwater, and sunlight. Kānehunamokū is the island of Kāne. Kānehoalani is the ruler of the heavens.

Kānehekili is the god of thunder. It is said that in a thunderstorm, hunchbacked figures may be seen in the clouds. Indeed, if one looks to the heavens during such an event, he may see the billowing figures creeping across the sky shadowed in the black clouds. But silence is the law of Kānehekili, and all persons should lie face down and make no sound during this time.

When Kāne appears in a worshipper's dream, he is in his imposing human form with feet standing upon the earth and his head touching the clouds. One side of his body is white, and the other side is black. The last ruling chief of Maui, Kahekili, claimed Kānehekili as his ancestor and was tattooed on one side of his body to show his relation to the god of thunder.

Kinolau of Kāne include kō (sugarcane), 'ohe (bamboo), and the pueo.

KANALOA

The ocean god is Kanaloa, who creates the tides with each inhale and exhale. Followers of Kanaloa believe that he can heal those who are suffering under a kahuna's spell.

As the gods Kāne and Kanaloa traveled together around the islands in their human forms, Kāne would thrust his kauila staff into the ground to open up new springs so that they always have fresh water for their 'awa. Many of these springs still exist today. His kinolau are the he'e (octopus), and a medicinal herb called 'ala'ala pū loa.

The Night of Muku

In 2014, I made the acquaintance of a young filmmaker named Kenji Lee. He is the son of my hula sister. He explained that he was interested in interviewing me for a personal project.

We planned to film in the evening at a few spots in Wai'anae, where I bring my tours. Kenji invited friends and family members to join us, and we headed out to the western end of the island. Because we had planned a simple interview, I did not exercise proper care and attention to avoid committing any unknown offense. I failed to check the moon phase for the night.

Coming from Kapolei, the weather was clear and calm, and the drive was pleasant, with little traffic since it was late in the evening. Everyone carpooled, following my vehicle as the darkness slowly blanketed the west coast. Finally, we parked across the street from Kāneana Cave, our first stop. In a strange twist, we were surprised by a deluge of pelting rain as soon as we exited our vehicles. The wind started to pick up, so we hurried across the street to the confines of Kāneana.

As we stood at the mouth of the cave, just under shelter from the rain, each of us felt the space's palpable energy. I offered a chant before we entered, announcing myself and our intentions. Compared to the deluge we had just walked through, the cave was warm, but any comfort for those in our group was short-lived after I shared the stories of the haunted cave and we stepped back outside.

Upon departing the cave, we headed toward the end of the road and stopped at Keawa'ula. It was still raining, and the strong winds now made it uncomfortable. Kenji wanted to continue filming, and I raised my voice so everyone could hear me. I talked about the legends of the area and the purported night marchers' trail that comes down from the mountain.

The experience at Keawaʻula, while not quite as frightening as the cave, was interesting. At the end of my last story, the wind stopped howling, and the rain eased up to a mere drizzle. We made our way back to our cars and remarked on the strange change in the weather. While her friends were too nervous to talk about their own experiences, a young woman told me her back was burning. She turned around and pulled up her shirt to reveal a myriad of swirling red scratches all over her back. She felt weird for most of the night, she said, and admitted that she used to see ghosts as a child. These scratches were unusual for her, though.

Driving back to Kapolei, we saw rocks that had fallen onto the road near the cave we'd previously visited. Across the street were strewn branches of trees. But it wasn't until we got home that I realized my horrible mistake. This event was meant to be just an interview, and I failed to take notice of the moon phase for that night. I brought this group out on the night of Muku without the proper and essential precautions. The night of the gods is not one to be out playing the fool's game.

WHEN DO THEY MARCH?

My mother's family says that na huaka'i pō march on the last four moon phases, Kāne, Lono, Mauli, and Muku.

Pukui tells us that the night of Kāne, the 27th night of the lunar month is when spirits of departed chiefs march over the pathways they trod in life.

In her collection of stories, Hawaiian Mythology, Martha Beckwith states that the phantom night marchers are seen on the sacred nights of Kū, Kāne, Lono, and Kanaloa. She also says that they may be seen during the day if the procession means to welcome the soul of a dying relative.

Kepelino gives us a little more detail when he says, "The time for the march is between half after seven when the sun has actually set and about two in the morning before dawn breaks. It may occur on one of the nights of the gods; on Kū, Akua, Lono, Kāne, or on the nights of Kāloa."

Additionally, Kepelino says the parade may come when a chief has just died or will pass away soon. The family might not notice the procession, but a neighbor might see it and know that the ali'i had gone on to be with his ancestors.

Witnesses have claimed to see processions of Menehune on nights of Akua, the full moon, and either Hoku or Mahealani. Others have been said to witness a woman's march on the night of Hua. In addition, there are many accounts of seeing the night marcher procession on anniversaries of certain events.

According to the above information about the moon phases, three nights are dedicated to Kāne, with one night specifically sacred to this god. There are also eight nights dedicated to Kū, Lono, and Kanaloa. The night before the full moons is Hua, and of course, the full moons, of Akua, Hoku, and Māhealani. The time of sacred ritual for all islands is Māhealani.

Sacred, high-born aliʻi would march at night to avoid disrupting the lives of commoners. Sightings have also been reported during the day and night when a chief or a family member dies and on anniversaries of events like the Makahiki.

If we rely on the information given by our kūpuna and our scholars, we see that several nights and days are prime for night marcher sightings. However, not everyone sees these marches all the time.

Historically, processions and most sacred events in ancient Hawaiʻi happened during specific conditions. Our ancestors did not only rely on the moon phases; the conditions of the environment had to be just right as well. There could be no sound from humans or animals, no bird calls or scurrying of rats, no twisting clouds or shooting stars, no rain from the heavens or fire on land. Kāhuna were always watchful for hōʻailona to decide whether the gods looked favorably upon them and whether the event or procession could continue. Inclement weather or anything out of place may signify that their plans should not proceed.

It would be understandable to think that the conditions of the immediate environment, including the moon phase, would have to mimic that of the original procession, which would dictate whether the ʻoiʻo, the repeated parade of the spirits of the dead, would march.

☽ ○ ☾

Chapter 5
Ho'alo i ka Huaka'i Pō
To avoid the Night Marchers

Although the reasons for processions may differ and the nights in which the phantoms march vary, one part of the legend often remains the same. Upon encountering the ghostly procession, it would be in your best interest to get out of the way as quickly as possible. Otherwise, your life may be forfeit. If you are fortunate enough to have an ancestor or an 'aumakua within the procession who recognizes you and is willing to claim you as a descendant and plead for your life, you may survive. It may also help if you know and are able to recite your family genealogy in hopes that a relative or an 'aumakua amongst the group will claim you as well.

Marchers in Makaha

In 1991, I participated in a community college production about the history of the Wai'anae coast from ancient times until today. To give our cast of forty individuals a more authentic experience beyond a paper script, we learned hula from Kumu Hula, Vicky Holt Takamine. Additionally, we camped overnight on the beach at Pokai Bay, where, during our short stay, long-time residents came to share their knowledge and history of the area. The experience was very fulfilling.

Late that Saturday afternoon, a woman we called Aunty Ronnie brought us out in groups on a canoe to teach us how to paddle correctly. We learned how to handle ourselves in case the canoe capsized and how to right the canoe and empty the excess water. I loved it, it was hard work, but it was also invigorating and a lot of fun.

Later, Aunty Ronnie approached me and asked me to follow her to Kū'īlioloa heiau.

"We go talk," she said.

At the point just beyond the heiau, overlooking the great expanse of the sea, she spread her variety-store grass mat over a patch of sand, and we sat. She removed a flask from her oblong cigarette case, took a couple of long sips, and then returned it to her case.

"I live at Makaha Plantation on the third floor, right down the road from Kāne'aki Heiau. Always, always, there were night marchers coming down the valley and through Kāne'aki and the gated community. I heard the procession went through the resort too, but for sure, they come through where I live."

The energy at the heiau behind us seemed to change, and the ambient noise seemed to quiet down. I re-adjusted myself and settled into the spot where I sat.

"Wow," I whispered.

"The first night," Aunty Ronnie began, "was two in the morning. I woke up to go to the bathroom, and the second I opened my bedroom door, I was overcome with the really stink smell of sulfur. I almost threw up. It was so bad. At the same time, my whole apartment was filled with this noise, this deep noise of pahu drums pounding and pounding. It made my eardrums hurt. I made it as far as my kitchen when I felt his large hand grab me from the back of my head and force me down to my kitchen floor. It held me there, flat and splayed out. Even then, I saw huge feet marching on and on for more than an hour right through my kitchen. I knew it was night marchers because of all the stories I had heard so many times. Just when the procession was done, the hand that held me to the floor let me go but right before then, this voice whispered in my ear, 'Kaleiopuʻu.'"

I took a deep breath and asked nervously, "Oh man, what happened after that?"

Aunty Ronnie stared out into the sunset. Her eyes were beginning to fill with tears. "I told my father the next day about what happened, and he cried. He confirmed that night marchers came through my place and that the procession came from the top of Makaha valley and right through the places I just told you about. What really made him cry was when I told him about the name that was whispered in my ear. He said that hand that held me to the floor? That was an ancestor who was part of the night marcher procession. He recognized me and held me down for my own protection until the marchers passed. Right before the hand of the night marcher let me go, he identified himself by telling me our ancient family name. He was Kaleiopuʻu."

$$\text{☽ ○ ☾}$$

If you cannot outrun them, you do not know your genealogy, and no one in the phantom army can speak for you, you may escape certain death if you remove all of your clothing and lie face upwards, spread eagle, with your eyes closed in hopes that the phantom army will find you insane and that this shame may result in your life spared. Some legends say that, after removing your clothing, you should urinate and rub the urine all over your body so that the night marchers will find you too disgusting to bother.

There are a few different stories about what one is supposed to do when the night marchers are coming. Of course, as repeated within this writing, getting out of the way is the primary means of survival. However, what happens if your home or business is built on top of a night marcher path, making escape impossible?

Jason Lindo's grandfather, George K. Spencer, was a retired building inspector who was often called to read the Mahele documents. He could tell where the night marcher trails were. If a house were mistakenly built on or near a night marchers' path, George would advise people to plant ki, the ti plant, around their homes to help the night marchers detour around their properties.

It would be most prudent to determine first if the property you plan to build on contains a night marcher path and then make adjustments to your plans. Diligent research into Hawaiian history of the area and discussions with the neighbors will be helpful. With an influx of non-believers, there seem to be more people who refuse to acknowledge Hawaiian customs and write them off as mere superstition. People tend to neglect the spiritual history of a particular site when they want to build their homes or buildings. This is quite understandable when given the cost of land in Hawai'i. Who wants to spend a near fortune on property and then be told they shouldn't build anything on it?

In the last several years, I've been called to homes and businesses with the question, "Can you make them go away, or can we somehow divert the path of the night marchers so that we can live or work here without fear?"

The night marchers, spirits of ancient warriors, were here long before us. Instead of a futile attempt to cleanse a home or business to get rid of them, it would be easier to understand the history and make adjustments to the space.

Since the traditions of the ʻoiʻo and the reasons for their march differ from place to place, there is no "cure-all" when it comes to dealing with them or even attempting to live with them peacefully. However, there is a belief that planting a row of ti plants may divert the night marchers if you find that your house sits upon their path.

Cordyline fruticosa, also known as the Hawaiian kī or ti plant, has many cultural, medicinal, and spiritual uses. While the actual origin of using ti leaves in protecting against spirits, lifting kapu, and calling down blessings from above is lost, the knowledge of performing such acts is quite common among the people of Hawaiʻi. It is well known that parts of the ti plant are used in sacred ceremonies under the kānāwai akua, the law of the gods.

Following are some traditional uses of ti as explained by Pukui:

"A person carrying food, especially pork, after dark was thought to be endangered by hungry ghosts. Ti leaves tied around the food gave full protection. The ʻawa for offering the spirit in a seance was prepared and served on ti leaves. Ti gave protection when a menstruating woman had to cross Pele's domain. Ti was also used to exorcise an evil spirit, especially when the possessed (noho) one was a child or unable to talk."

In 1893, J. S. Emerson wrote:

"A well-to-do Hawaiian of my acquaintance, after building an expensive frame house, was warned by the kahuna not to live in it on pain of death until the flowers should appear on a hedge of ti plants with which he was directed to surround the house. For a whole year or more, he was obliged to live in his old grass house while the new one stood empty, waiting for the hedge to grow and the flowers to bloom, making it habitable."

Diversion

In the quiet town of Lāʻie, a prominent man of the community stood waiting outside his front door. A mutual acquaintance had set up a meeting between this man and me, and I was several minutes late. Not being in the habit of driving out to the North Shore, I always seem to misjudge the traffic. As I pulled into the driveway, I saw the impatient look on his face, so I quickly parked and rushed up to shake his hand. I apologized and asked if he wanted to reschedule, but he waved off my question and had me follow him into his home.

The tall Hawaiian man wasn't in the mood for pleasantries as he led me to a large bedroom at the far end of his house. On one side of the room was a regular double bunk bed with two teenage boys sitting on the bottom bunk, and directly across from it was a triple bunk bed with one teen girl sitting on the bottom bunk and a younger girl in the middle. A third young girl was sitting on a chair near her sisters. The man introduced them as his children.

"Tell him," the man said. He was looking at the children but pointing his finger toward me.

The boys explained that on a few nights every month, some unseen force would violently push the beds and furniture toward one side of the room, usually while the children were still sleeping. Other times, the same invisible force would pull them out of their beds by their feet and drag them across the floor, kicking and screaming. They could see no person or figure doing these things, but they happened nonetheless. The problem started just a few months before, seemingly out of the blue. The children were scared, and the parents didn't know what else to do.

I asked what happened right before the beds moved or the kids were pulled out of bed, and the children said they had only been sleeping. None of them remembered any particular sound or scent. They could not recall anything when asked about specific dreams before the occurrence.

I looked around the house, and then the man showed me around outside. Standing at the edge of the street, facing the home, I noticed that along the left side of the property, a thick row of tall, aged ti plants grew, extending just past the edge of the back of the house. A beautiful, lush growth, full of green and yellow leaves, stretching above the eaves of the roof, they had stalks nearly as thick as my wrist. On the right side of the house was a long strip of dirt mirroring the length of the ti plants that grew on the left side. I asked the man what happened there, and he said that his wife didn't like the ti plants, so she dug them all up as she planned to grow flowers instead. That right side of the home was the location of the children's room. It turns out that the activity in the room began shortly after their mom pulled out all the ti plants.

I explained to the man that it sounded like the house he was living in might be in the path of the night marchers. The original builders probably knew that hence the rows of mature ti plants. By removing the plants, he and his wife also removed the protection from the phantom army. His Hawaiian blood may have protected the children by moving them out of the way during the procession, but the activity won't stop until they replanted the row of ti.

The man scoffed and said that while he acknowledged the Hawaiian superstition, his religion prevented him from believing it. He exclaimed that God would protect him but asked me to perform a Hawaiian blessing over his home to make his wife feel better.

I can't force my beliefs on anyone, and after blessing his home, I strongly encouraged him to reconsider replacing the ti plants. A few months later, I ran into the person who originally put me in contact with the man in Lā'ie. I found out that the man and his wife still decided to remove the remaining ti plants on the left side of the property. Unfortunately, the terrifying activity had not stopped, and the family moved out shortly after. The house itself, as I understand, seems to change tenants quite frequently.

☽ ○ ☾

Sometimes it might be impossible to plant ti to divert a night marchers' path, as would be the case in the city. For example, the attorneys in Downtown Honolulu who believed their security cameras captured the night marchers on video were on the 23rd floor and were unable to plant anything.

In their case, I suggested that they allow at least potted ti plants in rows to guide the marchers through an unused space. Also, if any office furniture were disturbed by what might be night marchers, it would be prudent to rearrange the furniture so that it doesn't impede the flow of the ʻoiʻo. Other than the images on video, nothing else in this office was disturbed, so I explained that the only thing left to do was leave them be and ensure no one is working there at night.

No matter when or how you experience the night marchers' phenomenon, the only thing that will truly save you is not being present when it happens

☽ ○ ☾

Chapter 6
Na Huaka'i Oko'a
Other Processions

Although the Night Marchers, the processions of the souls of gods, warriors, and ali'i, are a uniquely Hawaiian phenomenon, there are accounts from people around the globe who have claimed to see other ghostly processions.

Sometimes those processions are similar to the night marchers, but their purposes differ from region to region. Some have said that the parade of the dead in Europe comprised of sinners and those who were damned, marching in punishment for their wrongdoings in life. Others have said that the procession of the dead is an omen of death. Still, others believe that the marches are a recasting of the Wild Hunt phenomenon to fit the beliefs, scenery, and narrative of other regions.

Processions and parades are not unique to Hawai'i. Our research included finding similarities between the legend of the night marchers and other processions of the dead.

Following are a few examples of different processions around the world.

☽ ○ ☾

WAGON TRAINS – AMERICAN MIDWEST

In early 2015, a woman on my tour described seeing a long train of wagons traveling in the distance on the plains of the American Midwest when she was a girl. Although her friend hadn't seen it, she was sure she had witnessed a full train of horses and covered wagons in front of her. There are many instances of people seeing processions of wagon trains across the continental U.S.

At Fort de Chartres, in Southern Illinois, near the east bank of the Mississippi River, locals are said to have witnessed a funeral procession carrying the body of a man who was killed and buried under cover of darkness. Around midnight on July 4, 1889, two women saw the funerary procession and nearly forty wagons, with a low wagon at the end carrying a casket. Remarkably, with the horses stomping while pulling the wagons and the riders seeming to talk to each other, the women could not hear any sound aside from the wind. Since then, the procession is only seen when the 4th of July falls on a Friday.

$$) \ O \ ($$

PERE DAGOBERT DE LONGUORY – LOUISIANA, US

Before the latter half of the 18th century, the vast territory of Central North America, known as La Luisiane, was claimed and controlled by France. During the Seven Years' War, however, France ceded the territory to Spain under the terms of the secret Treaty of Fontainebleau in 1762. French colonists in New Orleans were less than pleased as they feared that Spanish trade restrictions would ruin the local economy. In 1767, Spain attempted to finally replace the French authority in New Orleans, resulting in a rebellion led by urban elites and rural militias. Two years later, Spain sent military governor Alejandro O'Reilly with a flotilla of 23 armed ships to restore Spanish authority. Five of the leading conspirators were executed at Fort St. Charles and, according to legend, were denied traditional Catholic burial rites. The families of the slain men solicited the aid of Père Dagobert de Longuory, a Capuchin monk who became the priest of St. Louis Cathedral. According to legend, Père Dagobert transported the bodies for interment at the St. Peter Street Cemetery, avoiding detection by the Spanish guard.

One may hear the sandaled footsteps of the priest and his helpers on certain foggy mornings as he repeats his miracle procession.

☽ ○ ☾

HYAKKI YAGYŌ - JAPAN

There is a legend in Japan that tells of a Night Parade of One Hundred Demons. General descriptions say that on certain nights, a horde of supernatural beings referred to as oni and yōkai walk the earth in a terrifying procession. If one is unfortunate enough to come across this horrible parade, he will either perish or be spirited away by the yōkai. Some legends state that a spell, either written or chanted, will save you from a terrible fate, while others say that remaining indoors or avoiding the procession entirely is your only hope of salvation.

A story by Richard Gordon Smith, printed in 1908, shares one legend of the Hyakki Yagyō. It tells of a place not far from Fushimi, near Kyoto, a few hundred years ago called the Shozenji Temple. This temple was said to be so severely haunted that the priests deserted the temple in fear, and it was allowed to rot and fall into ruin.

One year, a lone priest on a pilgrimage who was a stranger to the area came upon the temple's ruins. Not knowing its history, he entered the temple seeking refuge from the cold weather instead of continuing his journey to Fushimi. The old priest planned to spend the night in a dry room and then resume his journey in the morning. The man made his bed in one of the smaller rooms that showed the least amount of disrepair. After eating his meal, the priest said his prayers and lay down to rest while the wind howled through the old buildings and the rain fell in torrents upon the beaten roof. Although he tried, it was just too cold for the priest to sleep, so he lay awake, shivering through the night.

Somewhere beyond the walls of the small room, the man heard strange and unnatural noises and decided to investigate. In the main building, he found Hyakki Yagyō, a procession of a hundred ghosts. The spirits filled the room, fighting, wrestling, and dancing. Though the priest was afraid and alarmed, he was also curious and stood to watch for a while. After a few moments, more nefarious-looking spirits seemed to arrive. The priest ran back, locked himself in the small room, and spent the rest of the night saying prayers for the souls of the dead.

As soon as it was light enough to see, and although the weather was still wet, the priest hurriedly made his way to Fushimi and told the villagers what he'd witnessed. The news spread so quickly and widely that Shozenji Temple was soon known as the most haunted temple in the territory.

Another legend explains that the residents of Kyoto once abandoned their old antiques on the side of the road after a big cleanup. These antiques were angry at their humans for abandoning them and transformed into yōkai spirits seeking revenge on the people.

Nowadays, Taishogun Shopping Street, also known as "Ichijo Yōkai Street" in northern Kyoto is believed to be a boundary line between the human world and that of the spirits. Each year, on the third Saturday of October, the town hosts the Hyakki Yagyō, the night parade when all the participants dress up in elaborate yōkai costumes.

☽ ○ ☾

PANCHABHĀYA - NEPAL

In the Himalayan region of Nepal, Panchabhāya folklore is widespread and has influenced place names throughout the area. The Panchabhāya is a procession of five or more spirits, often dressed in white. The dead are said to ride horses and cross the countryside from sunset to sunrise, following the same route every night. If a person were unlucky enough to meet this procession, they would become sick or even die.

In some stories, the procession is preceded by a black dog. It is believed that if someone is able to place himself between the dog and the ghostly marchers, he can catch the first spirit of the procession and ask it for whatever he wants. Only when the ghost fulfills the man's wishes will he be able to continue wandering with the procession.

☽ ○ ☾

BAHADUR SHAH ZAFAR ~ INDIA

The Red Fort is located in Delhi, India, and served as the primary residence of the Mughal Emperors.

The power of the last Mughal, Bahadur Shah Zafar, was reduced to preside over the dwindling empire in Delhi during the 19th century. During this time, the British-controlled East India Company had come to rule large areas of India with its private armies, exercising military power and seizing administrative functions.

The British allowed the emperor a pension and the authority to collect taxes and maintain a small military force in Delhi. However, Bahadur Shah Zafar had immersed himself in Urdu poetry and calligraphy and showed little interest in managing the state. Zafar's poetry was primarily about love and mysticism, with Delhi as the backdrop.

During the rebellion of 1857, Indian regiments acclaimed Zafar their leader, despite his reservations. British forces surrounded the family and brutally killed numerous members of the Zafar family. In 1858, Zafar, his wife, and their two remaining sons were exiled to Rangoon, Burma (also known as Yangon, Myanmar). While imprisoned, pen, ink, and paper were prohibited. Guards visited the family daily in the morning and evening as part of surveillance. Still, the public was not allowed to meet them, and servants could gain access only via a pass issued by the European officer.

Already 83 years old at the time of his exile, Bahadur Shah Zafar's health declined considerably while imprisoned, and he died in November 1862. His wife, Zinat Mahal, followed his death four years later.

While Zafar and his wife were imprisoned and buried in Myanmar, it is said that he left his heart in Delhi. People of Delhi believe that on Thursday nights, a ghost procession led by the last Mughal king and his beautiful consort comes out of the primary Lahori Gate, silently walks around the Red Fort, and then returns to the main gate before quietly disappearing.

$$\mathcal{D} \bigcirc \mathbb{C}$$

THE WILD HUNT ~ EUROPE

For centuries, villagers all over Europe have described a phenomenon that has continued to the present day. On long winter nights, the sounds of hundreds of souls passing through the forests and towns are carried on the winds. People encountering this procession might be abducted into the underworld or the fairy kingdom, or their spirits could be coerced during sleep and carried away to join the procession.

Known commonly as the Wild Hunt or Infernal Hunt, the stories still inspire poets and writers. Typically, the Wild Hunt is a group of ghostly hunters passing over the land with a host of foot soldiers and knights, some bloody and worn, and some carrying their own heads.

From Ireland and England to Scandinavia to Germany to Italy and all countries in between, the Wild Hunt has become a catch-all term for many different ghostly processions throughout the ages. The exact origins of the hunt are unknown, and tales vary depending on where the host of the damned is seen. This wild procession can be made up of elves, fairies, or the dead. The leader may often be a notable, legendary figure or even an unidentified lost soul or spirit. Sometimes the Wild Hunt is thought to be an omen of some catastrophe or plague or the death of the person who witnessed it.

The first story I've ever heard of the Wild Hunt was that of King Herla and his band of hunters.

One day long ago, the king of dwarves approached the Briton King to announce that he would attend Herla's wedding. In return, Herla would attend the Dwarf King's wedding on the same day, one year later. King Herla agreed, and the Dwarf King swiftly departed.

True to his word, the Dwarf King showed up with his people at the wedding of King Herla, bearing extravagant gifts and enough food for everyone. Herla's guests were impressed and praised the dwarves for their hospitality. At the end of the night, Herla was reminded of his commitment to attend the Dwarf King's wedding in exactly one year, then the entire party of dwarves left to make it home before sunrise.

On the night of his first wedding anniversary, King Herla kept his promise. He and his men, carrying adequate supplies for a sufficient repayment, entered the dwarves' lair through a cave in a cliff and proceeded to engage in the festivities for three whole days. When it was time to leave, the generous Dwarf King presented King Herla with gifts of horses, dogs, and every apparatus meant for hunting. Finally, the Dwarf King handed Herla a hound with a strict warning that none of his party must dismount until the dog leaped from Herla's arms to the earth. With that, the Britons left to return home.

Shortly after leaving the dwarves' cave, Herla and his men came upon a farmer and asked about his queen. The man could hardly understand the king and stated thus. He informed the king that he had heard of a queen by that name from long ago, and tales say that her husband, King Herla, disappeared from the land one year after their marriage.

He said, "We Saxons have lived in this kingdom for two hundred years after driving out the old Britons."

During this conversation, some of the king's men dismounted their horses and immediately turned to dust. King Herla, realizing the reason for this and remembering the Dwarf King, warned the rest to remain on their horses as the dog had not yet leaped to the ground himself.

To his amazement and sadness, King Herla believed he'd only stayed in the underground kingdom of the dwarves for three days. But time had passed much more swiftly in the human world, and he realized he'd been gone for centuries. For this, it is said that King Herla and his band remain cursed to travel from one land to the next in a sad, quiet procession.

While this is not the only narrative of the Wild Hunt, it's the one that has stuck in my mind since childhood. Several authors offer interpretations of this tale and have done much to collect and analyze the many different stories of the Wild Hunt.

☽ ○ ☾

DIE TOTENPROZESSION ~ SWITZERLAND

There is a phenomenon that comes out of Switzerland called Die Totenprozession, The Procession of the Dead. Some believe this procession may predict the death of the people in the parade or the person who witnesses it. The seer would recognize some people in the procession, and they would soon die in the order in which they marched.

Also called Bergen Gratzug (Ridge Train) or a Symphonie on certain mountains, when such a procession passes, one might hear a dull murmuring, the sound of marching, and the unmistakable sound of drumming and whistling. Soon, there may be music, weeping, and laughing voices. When the ridge train marches, one should always stand or lie down off the path because the dead must not do any harm there. However, if one remains in the way or lies under the path, the dead will have power over him.

The story of one pastor who witnessed the Totenprozession says that the man was getting dressed and had just put on one stocking when he heard a crowd outside. He rushed to the window, and looking out, he saw a large procession walking past, praying loudly. As the pastor of his small town, he knew all the men, women, and children in the march. Then, at the very end, was a man wearing one stocking while the other stocking he carried under his arm. When the procession was over, the pastor took his stocking from his armpit and put it on. He said he then knew who in his community would die of the plague and that he would be the last. And so it happened.

LA SANTA COMPAÑA - IBERIAN PENINSULA, SOUTHWEST EUROPE

The region of Galicia, Northwest Spain, Portugal, and other areas in the Iberian Peninsula, are the settings for the deeply-rooted belief of La Santa Compaña, The Holy Company. Over the years, the tale has even made its way to Mexico as La Santa Compaña, La Guestia, or La Estadea. The legend is so old that no one can say where it actually began, but people have still claimed to see the Holy Company in recent years.

There may be many versions of La Santa Compaña, but most agree that it is a procession of souls that wander through villages wearing long, white hooded cloaks and whose duty it is to announce one's death and visit the homes where death may be due.

My friend, José Beltrán, describes Galicia as "A land full of mystique and mystery. Its culture is basically Celtic, and the whole region feels, at times, like a rather spooky place: lots of dense forests, gray skies, fog, and in autumn and winter, it can get really dark out there. It is really easy to get lost if you stray from the well-trod path through one of those deep oak forests that dot the mountainous countryside."

La Santa Compaña, this Holy Company, this procession of the dead, is said to march in a long line, two by two, in their hooded shrouds carrying candles. A line of lights, the candles held by ghostly hands, is usually the only thing that is seen unless one is sensitive to the otherworldly or was mistakenly anointed by a priest with the oil used for the last rites.

The presence of the procession is announced in subtle ways. Though not visible to most people, it is said that the approach of La Santa Compaña can be "felt." Animals in the area either fall silent or run away. There is a faint sound of prayers or funerary songs or little bells getting closer, and the smell of melted wax fills the air.

Leading the ghostly group is the Estadea, the soul of a living person. Some say the Estadea is cursed to lead the procession every night. Others say that the astral body of the cursed Estadea lies in a coffin carried by the mournful dead. This goes on night after night. The Estadea grows progressively weaker until the body dies and the soul joins the procession or until he finds someone to take his place, freeing him from his ultimate doom.

What can you do if you are in the path of the Santa Compaña? Naturally, upon the first sign, the first bit of advice is often the best: Run! If you cannot run, several things are said to be sufficient protection against the Santa Compaña. Different sources will give different lists, but they all seem to have a similar absolute solution. When La Santa Compaña is near, the best protection is throwing yourself on the ground, face down, never looking up, and remaining motionless until the entire procession of the dead has passed.

As a collector of ghost stories from places and cultures all over the world, the legend of La Santa Compaña seems to be the most similar to Hawaii's Night Marchers, especially since people still report seeing them in this modern day.

After discussing the similarities between Hawaii's Night Marchers and La Santa Compaña, my friend José says, "I would like to tell you of another amusing point of contact between Hawai'i and Spain. The standard term for 'goosebumps' in Spanish is 'piel de gallina,' which translates to… chicken skin."

☽ ○ ☾

Helu Pō

Hawaiian Moon Phases

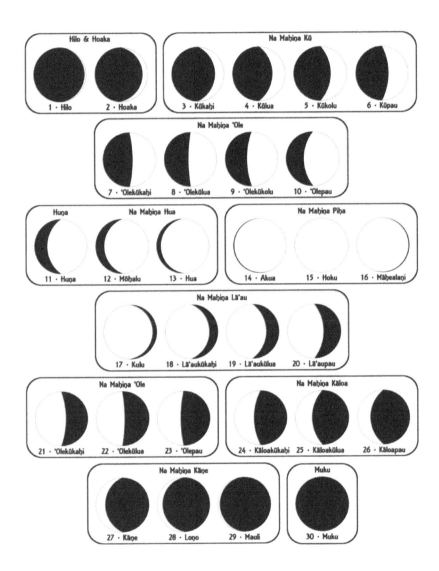

List of Kiʻi Pohaku
Petroglyphs

GLOSSARY OF HAWAIIAN WORDS

While many Hawaiian words have more than one meaning, the definitions below are of words as they apply to the specific context within this book.

ahi makaihuwaʻa - the innumerable fires of the divine ancestors of the night

ahupuaʻa - land division usually extending from the uplands to the sea

ʻahuʻula - feather cloak, usually red or yellow trimmed with black or green, formerly worn by high chiefs or kings

ʻai kapu - to eat under taboo; to observe eating taboos

akua - a god, goddess, spirit, ghost, devil, image, idol, corpse; divine, supernatural, godly

akua kapu - the kapu of an aliʻi whose back was sacred that no person must follow behind him

ʻalaʻalapuloa - *Waltheria indica*; medicinal herb

ʻālaʻapapa - a type of ancient hula

aliʻi - chief, chiefess, ruler, king, queen

alokapu - the kapu of an aliʻi whose face is sacred that no person could pass before him

ʻaumakua - family or personal gods, deified ancestors who might assume the shape of animals, clouds, or plants.

ʻaumākua - plural of ʻaumakua

'awa - *Piper methysticum;* also Kava, a shrub, native to Pacific islands, the root being the source of a drink of the same name used in ceremonies, prepared by chewing or pounding, the particles were mixed with water and strained, also used medicinally

bumbai - a local "pidgin" term meaning otherwise, or else, later on, soon

'e'epa - extraordinary, abnormal, peculiar, as persons with miraculous powers

'eho'eho - rock-like babies possibly the result of mortals producing with akua

Ha'a - the hairless 'olohe people of Maui

haku 'ōhi'a - main image in a heiau made from the 'ōhi'a tree

halau - hula school

hale - house, building

Hale Nauā - a group of kahuna which, in Kamehameha's time, scrutinized the genealogical qualifications of those who claimed relationship to the chiefs, and in Kalākaua's time, sought to revive elements of Hawaiian culture that were becoming lost with the passage of time and promoted the advancement of modern sciences, art, and literature

he'e - octopus

heiau - Hawaiian place of worship, shrine

helu pō - list of the Hawaiian moon phases

hō'ailona - sign or portent

ho'i - marriage of a chief with the daughter of a brother or sister

hō'ike a ka pō - to receive revelations in a dream

huaka'i pō - traveling in the night, also a common name of the night marchers

hula - Hawaiian dance form accompanied by 'oli (chant) or mele (song)

humuhumunukunukuapua'a - trigger fish with a snout like a pig

'ilio - dog

imu - underground oven

'io - Hawaiian hawk, endemic and endangered

ipu hokiokio - the whistling gourd

kahuna - Hawaiian priest, sorcerer, magician, wizard, minister, expert in any profession

kāhuna - plural of kahuna

kākāola - visible spirit of a living person

kalo - *Colocasia esculenta;* taro, a kind of aroid cultivated since ancient times for food

kanaka - human being, man, person

kānāwai akua - law or edict of the god or gods

kāne - male, husband, male sweetheart, man

kaona - double meaning; metaphorical meaning

kapa - tapa, a fabric made from wauke (*Broussonetia papyrifera*) or māmaki (*Pipturus albidus*) bark

kapu - sacred, holy, consecrated

kapu loulu luakini - ceremonies for peace for duration and reign of the king

kapu moe - prostrating kapu in accordance with a chief's status; lying face down in their presence

kapu noho - sitting kapu in accordance with a chief's status; sitting in their presence

kauila - *Alphitonia ponderosa;* a native tree in the buckthorn family used for spears and mallets; also one of three kinds of trees on Mauna Loa, Moloka'i, that were rumored to be poisonous from that location alone, and used in black magic

kī- *Cordyline fruticosa;* also ti, a shrub very common on all islands; the leaves, called lai or laui, served as wrappers for food and as plates, and were also used for thatching, ceremonies and rituals

kihei - a cape; rectangular kapa garment worn over one shoulder and tied in a knot

ki'i - carved idol images

ki'i pohaku - petroglyphs

kinolau - the physical embodiments of a god, demi-god, or 'aumakua

kō - *Saccharum officinarum;* sugar cane

kohekohe - *Eleocharis erythropoda;* the tallest of the native
 spikerush

kukui - *Aleurites moluccana;* candlenut tree, the nuts
 containing oily kernels which were used for lights

kukuihaele - traveling lights; another name for night marchers

kuleana - right, privilege, concern, responsibility

kumu - teacher, tutor

kumu hula - hula teacher, source of hula

Kumulipo - name of the Hawaiian creation chant

kupuna - grandparent, ancestor, relative

kūpuna - plural of kupuna

'iwikuamo'o - near and trusted relative of a chief who attended
 to his personal needs and possessions, and executed
 family orders

Lē'ahi- Diamond Head, Honolulu, O'ahu

leina a ka 'uhane - leaping place of the spirits

lua a milu - the pit of Milu, the god of the underworld

luakini - heiau where ruling chiefs prayed and human
 sacrifices were offered

mahina - moon, month; moonlight

mahi'ole - feather helmet

Makahiki - ancient festival beginning about the middle of
 October and lasting about four months, with sports and
 religious festivities and kapu on war

makai - oceanside

Makali'i - the star cluster Pleiades

malo - male's loincloth

mauka - inland, towards the mountains

Menehune - legendary race of small people who worked at
    night, building fish ponds, roads, temples

moa - chicken

moe - to sleep, lie down; to lie in wait, ambush; to prostrate
    oneself, as before a chief

mokomoko - Hawaiian wrestling

mo'o - Hawaiian water spirit, lizard, serpent

mo'olelo - story, tale, myth, history, tradition

na huaka'i o ka pō - the travelers in the night, another name
    for night marchers

naha - bent, curved, bowed; union of a chief with his
    half-sister

na'u - mine

nī'au pi'o - the midrib arching on itself; offspring of the
    marriage of a high-born brother and sister, or half-brother
    and half-sister

niu - *Cocos nucifera;* coconut

noho - to sit; also possession of a medium by a spirit or god

'ohana - family

'ohe - *Schizostachyum glaucifolium;* bamboo

'ohe hanu ihe - the bamboo nose flute

'ōhi'a - *Metrosideros polymorpha;* variety of tree

'oi'o - procession of ghosts of a departed chief and his company; another name for night marchers

'ōlelo no'eau - Hawaiian proverbs

'oli - a chant, often with prolonged phrases chanted in one breath

'olopū - adze for cutting 'ōhi'a logs for ki'i images

pahu - drum

Papa'ena'ena - ancient temple of human sacrifice located on the slopes of present day Diamond Head

pō - night, darkness; the realm of the gods

Pō Kāne - the night of the god Kāne

po'okanaka - human head; a class of heiau that was created for human sacrifice

pū - large triton conch or helmet shell used for trumpets

pua'a - pig

pueo - owl

pule o'o - prayers so powerful, they ripen like fruit

Pu'uhonua - place of refuge, sanctuary, asylum, place of peace and safety

'uala - *Ipomea batatas;* variety of sweet potato

'uhane - soul, spirit, ghost

'ulu - *Artocarpus altilis;* breadfruit

ulua - certain species of crevalle, jack, or pompano, an important game fish and food item

wahine - woman, lady, wife

wauke - the paper mulberry, *Broussonetia papyrifera,* a small tree or shrub used to make kapa

REFERENCES

Abbott, Isabella Aiona. *La'au Hawai'i: Traditional Hawaiian Use of Plants*. Bishop Museum Press, 1992.

Alexander, William De Witt. *A Brief History of the Hawaiian People*. University Press of the Pacific, 2001.

Alia. "Santa Compaña: A Procession of Souls." *Follow the Camino*, 21 Aug. 2019, followthecamino.com/blog/santa-compana-a-procession-of-souls/.

Apple, Russ, and Peg Apple. "Victim of the Night Marchers." *The Honolulu Star-Bulletin*, 5 Sept. 1980, p. A13, www.newspapers.com/image/271862675.

Armand, Fabio, et al. "Death Divination within a Non-Delusional Myth: The Procession of the Dead from the Alps to Himalayas...When a Theoria of 'Phantom-Bodies' Meets Its Neural Veridiction Theory." *Academia.edu*, 2016, www.academia.edu/51280574/Death_Divination_Within_a_Non_Delusional_Myth_The_Procession_of_the_Dead_from_the_Alps_to_Himalayas_When_a_Theoria_of_Phantom_Bodies_Meets_Its_Neural_Veridiction_Theory.

Ashdown, Inez MacPhee. *Ke Alaloa o Maui*. Kama'aina Historians, 1971.

Auerbach, Loyd. *Ghost Hunting: How to Investigate the Paranormal*. Ronin Pub., 2004.

Auerbach, Loyd. *Hauntings and Poltergeists: a Ghost Hunter's Guide*. Ronin Pub., 2004.

Barayuga, Debra. "Moanalua High at Ease after Blessing Ceremony." *Honolulu Star-Bulletin*, 4 Nov. 1998, pp. A3, https://www.newspapers.com/image/273939203/. Accessed 4 Jan. 2023.

Beckwith, Martha Warren. *Hawaiian Mythology*. University of Hawai'i Press, 1970.

Beckwith, Martha Warren. *The Kumulipo: a Hawaiian Creation Chant*. Univ. of Hawai'i Pr., 1951, *Ulukau.org*, www.ulukau.org/elib/collect/beckwit2/index/assoc/D0.di r/book.pdf.

Brown, Alan. *Ghosts Along the Mississippi River*. University Press of Mississippi, 2011.

Clark, John R. K. *Hawai'i Place Names: Shores, Beaches, and Surf Sites*. University of Hawai'i Press, 2002.

Collins, Sara, and Patrick McCoy. *Burial Treatment Plan for Burial Sites in the Mauna Kea Science Reserve and the Mauna Kea Access Road Corridor, Ka'ohe Ahupua'a, Hāmākua District, Island of Hawai'i*. Pacific Consulting Services, June 2014.

Cox, J. Halley, and Edward Stasack. *Hawaiian Petroglyphs*. Bishop Museum Press, 1990.

Crowe, Catherine. *The Night Side of Nature or Ghosts and Ghost Seers*. G. Routledge and Company, 1852, https://play.google.com/books/reader?id=sbM6AAAAcA AJ&hl=en&pg=GBS.PP4

Das, Sarat C. "A Ghost Funeral in Chandni Chowk." *Hindustan Times*, 29 May 2008, www.hindustantimes.com/delhi/a-ghost-funeral-in-chand ni-chowk/story-QPLv2cnA9fs1Ou0KoWS23H.html.

De Fries, Emma. "Malo-Clad Warriors Scare Off Workers." *The Honolulu Advertiser*, 31 Oct. 1971, pp. C4, https://www.newspapers.com/image/261095780/. Accessed 2 Mar. 2020.

Desha, Stephen, and Frances N. Frazier. *Kamehameha and His Warrior Kekūhaupi'o*. Kamehameha Schools Press, 2000.

Emerson, J. S. "Myth of Hiku and Kawelu." *Hawaiian Almanac and Annual for 1883*, vol. 9, 1983, pp. 36–39., http://hdl.handle.net/10524/657.

Emerson, J. S. "Some Hawaiian Beliefs Regarding Spirits." *Ninth Annual Report of the Hawaiian Historical Society*, 1902, pp. 15–17., play.google.com/books/reader?id=f8lJAQAAMAAJ&hl=en&pg=GBS.PP1.

Fornander, Abraham. *Hawaiian Antiquities and Folk-Lore.* Bishop Museum Press, 1918. http://ulukau.org/elib/collect/fornander5/index/assoc/D0.dir/book.pdf

"Ghost of Westkaemper Keeps Tabs on Supplies, Postal Employee Asserts." *The Honolulu Advertiser*, 26 Feb. 1925, pp. 1–2, www.newspapers.com/clip/16100102/ghost-of-postal-employee-story/.

Ginzburg, Carlo, et al. *The Night Battles: Witchcraft & Agrarian Cults in the Sixteenth & Seventeenth Centuries.* The Johns Hopkins University Press, 1992.

Gonser, James. *Capitol Ghost Stories - The Queen Helps a Child*, 24 Oct. 2007, hawaiihouseblog.blogspot.com/2007/10/capitol-ghost-stories-queen-helps-child.html.

Gowen, Herbert H. *The Napoleon of the Pacific: Kamehameha the Great.* AMS Press, 1977.

Grant, Glen. *Obake Files: Ghostly Encounters in Supernatural Hawai'i.* Mutual, 1996.

Handy, E. S. Craighill, et al. *Native Planters in Old Hawaii: Their Life, Lore, and Environment.* Bishop Museum Press, 1972.

"History of the Parapsychological Association." *The Parapsychological Association*, 25 Apr. 2010, parapsych. org/articles/1/14/history_of_the_parapsychological.aspx.

Hitt, Christine. "The Sacred History of Maunakea." *Honolulu Magazine*, 13 Apr. 2021, https://www.honolulumagazine.com/the-sacred-history-o f-maunakea/.

Ho'omanawanui, Ku'ualoha. "Hanohano Wailuanuiaho'āno: Remembering, Recovering, and Writing Place." *Hūlili: Multidisciplinary Research on Hawaiian Well-Being*, vol. 8, 2012, pp. 187–243.

Hosek, Linda. "New Land Divisions Mapped Out." *Honolulu Star-Bulletin*, 20 Apr. 1987, pp. A3, https://www.newspapers.com/image/273114183/. Accessed 2 Mar. 2020.

Hutton, Ronald. *The Witch: a History of Fear, from Ancient Times to the Present*. Yale University Press, 2018.

Ii, John Papa, et al. *Fragments of Hawaiian History*. Bishop Museum Press, 1959.

"Introduction to Kona Hema (South Kona)." *Hōnaunau Ola Mau Loa*, 2014, http://honaunau.org/introduction-to-kona-hema-south-ko na/.

Joesting, Edward. *Kauai: The Separate Kingdom*. University of Hawai'i Press, 1984.

Jordan, Dylan. "Four Real New Orleans Legends That Put Ghost Stories to Shame." *The Historic New Orleans Collection*, 15 Oct. 2018, www.hnoc.org/publications/first-draft/four-real-new-orle ans-legends-put-ghost-stories-shame.

Kamakau, Samuel Manaiakalani. *Ruling Chiefs of Hawaii*. Kamehameha Schools Press, 1992.

"Kanaloa." *Kumukahi*, Kamehameha Publishing, 2020, www.kumukahi.org/units/ke_ao_akua/akua/kanaloa.

"Kāne." *Kumukahi*, Kamehameha Publishing, 2020, www.kumukahi.org/units/ke_ao_akua/akua/kane.

Karpiel, Frank. "Notes & Queries, The Hale Naua Society." *Hawaiian Journal of History*, vol. 33, 1999, pp. 203–212.

Kepelino, and Martha Warren Beckwith. *Kepelino's Traditions of Hawaii*. Bishop Museum Press, 2007.

Kikuchi, William K. "Ka Pai Ki'i Mahu o Wailua:The Petroglyphs of Wailua, District of Lihu'e, Island of Kaua'i. Site 50-30-08-105A." *Rapa Nui Journal* , vol. 8, no. 2, 1 Jan. 1994, pp. 27–32., evols.library.manoa.hawaii.edu/server/api/core/bitstreams/043fde8f-b601-416a-9065-ee0dcbb17a3b/content. Accessed 20 Feb. 2023.

Kirch, Patrick Vinton, and Babineau Thérèse I. *Legacy of the Landscape: An Illustrated Guide to Hawaiian Archaeological Sites*. University of Hawai'i Press, 1996.

Krauss, Bob. "Hairstylist Has Good on Ghost." *The Honolulu Advertiser*, 27 Aug. 2000, pp. A25, https://www.newspapers.com/image/265854210/. Accessed 2 Mar. 2020.

"Kū." *Hawaii Alive* , Bishop Museum, 2020, hawaiialive.org/realms.php?sub=Wao%2BLani&treasure=340&offset=0.

"Ku." *Kumukahi*, Kamehameha Publishing, 2020, www.kumukahi.org/units/ke_ao_akua/akua/ku.

Lambeth, Harry. "Paliku, Famed Hawaiian Showplace, Now St. Stephen's Junior Seminary." *Honolulu Star-Bulletin*, 24 Oct. 1946, p. 12, https://www.newspapers.com/image/258404214/. Accessed 3 Mar. 2020.

Lecouteux, Claude. *Phantom Armies of the Night: the Wild Hunt and Ghostly Processions of the Undead*. Inner Traditions, 2011.

Lee, Georgia, and Edward Stasack. *Spirit of Place: The Petroglyphs of Hawaiʻi*. Easter Island Foundation, 2000.

Lee-Greig, Tanya L., and Hallet H. Hammat. *A Cultural Impact Assessment for the Proposed Olowalu Town Master Plan in Olowalu Ahupuaʻa, Lāhainā District, Island of Maui*. Olowalu Ahupuaʻa, Lahaina Disctrict, Mar. 2015.

"Lono." *Kumukahi*, Kamehameha Publishing, 2020, www.kumukahi.org/units/ke_ao_akua/akua/lono.

"Louisiana (New Spain)." *Wikipedia*, Wikimedia Foundation, 9 July 2020, en.wikipedia.org/wiki/Louisiana_(New_Spain).

Lucas, Carolyn. "Spooky Island Stories Abound." *Hawaii Tribune Herald*, 30 Oct. 2005, pp. A8, https://www.newspapers.com/image/557313965/. Accessed 2 Mar. 2020.

Luomala, Katharine. "Phantom Night Marchers in the Hawaiian Islands." *Pacific Studies*, vol. 7, no. 1, 1983, pp. 1–33., doi:https://contentdm.lib.byu.edu/digital/collection/PacificStudies/id/787.

Macrae, James. *With Lord Byron at the Sandwich Islands in 1825: Being Extracts from the MS. Diary of James Macrae, Scottish Botanist*. W.F. Wilson, 1922, Google Books, https://books.google.com/books?id=0j0jbbEotekC&printsec=frontcover&source=gbs_ge_summary_r&cad=0#v=onepage&q&f=false, Accessed 7 Jan. 2023.

Malo, David, and Nathaniel Bright Emerson. *Hawaiian Antiquities: (Moolelo Hawaii)*. Bernice P. Bishop Museum, 1951.

Maly, Kepa and Onaona Maly. *Ka Hana Lawaiʻa a Me Na Koʻa o Na Kai ʻEwalu: A History of Fishing Practices and Marine Fisheries of the Hawaiian Islands.* Kumu Pono Associates, 2003, *Ulukau,* ulukau.org/elib/collect/maly2/index/assoc/D0.dir/doc2.pdf.

"Mayor Tells of Past Pali Skeleton Finds." *The Honolulu Advertiser,* 10 July 1947, pp. 1–6, www.newspapers.com/image/259052279/. Accessed 12 Apr. 2018.

McGee, Oona. "Hyakki Yagyo: Night Parade of 100 Demons Scares Tourists in Kyoto." SoraNews24, 23 Oct. 2019, https://soranews24.com/2019/10/24/hyakki-yagyo-night-parade-of-100-demons-scares-tourists-in-kyoto%E3%80%90videos%E3%80%91/.

Mellen, George. "Wild Honey, Musings of a Kamaʻaina in Hawaii." *The Honolulu Star-Bulletin*, 27 Sept. 1940, p. 11, www.newspapers.com/image/25857275.

Miike, Lawrence H. *Water and the Law in Hawaiʻi.* University of Hawaiʻi Press, 2004, Google Books, https://play.google.com/books/reader?id=GZsBEAAAQBAJ&pg=GBS.PR2&hl=en, Accessed 6 June 2020.

Mitchell, Donald Dean. *Resource Units in Hawaiian Culture; a Series of Studies Covering Sixteen Important Aspects of Hawaiian Culture*. Kamehameha Schools, 1972.

Montell, William Lynwood. *Ghosts across Kentucky.* University Press of Kentucky, 2000.

"Na Moolelo O Kepakailiula." *Ka Nupepa Kuokoa*, 6 Apr. 1965, www.papakilodatabase.com/pdnupepa/?a=d&d=KNK18650406-01.2.4&srpos=1&e=06-04-1865-06-04-1865--en-20--1--txt-txIN%7ctxNU%7ctxTR-mahealani-------.

Penna, Tom. *Kilo Mahina Planner*, Hō Mai Ka Pono, 2020.

Pignataro, Anthony. "'Hawaii's Wounded Knee' – Remembering the Olowalu Massacre." *MauiTime, Mauis Best News, Information and Entertainment Site*, Maui Time, 20 Jan. 2016, https://mauitime.com/culture/history/hawaiis-wounded-knee-remembering-the-olowalu-massacre/.

Pukui, Mary Kawena, and Dietrich Varez. *'Olelo No'eau: Hawaiian Proverbs & Poetical Sayings*. Bishop Museum Press, 1983.

Pukui, Mary Kawena, et al. *Nānā i Ke Kumu: Look to the Source*. Hui Hanai, 1983.

Pukui, Mary Kawena, et al. *Place Names of Hawaii*. Rev. ed. University Press of Hawaii, 1984.

"Pu'ukohola Heiau National Historic Site." *NPSHistory.com*, 2014, http://npshistory.com/publications/puhe/index.htm.

Rice, William Hyde. *Hawaiian Legends*. Bishop Museum Press, 1977.

Ritz, Mary Kaye. "Spooked at the Seminary." *The Honolulu Advertiser*, 31 Oct. 2001, pp. F1-F3, https://www.newspapers.com/image/266764510/. Accessed 18 May 2001.

Safvi, Rana. "May 16, 1857: How a Massacre by Rebel Sepoys at the Red Fort Felled Bahadur Shah Zafar." *Scroll.in*, Scroll.in, 16 May 2017, scroll.in/article/835316/may-16-1857-how-a-massacre-by-rebel-sepoys-at-the-red-fort-felled-bahadur-shah-zafar.

Simonson, Mindy, and Hallett H. Hammatt. *Cultural Impact Assessment for the Thirty Meter Telescope (TMT) Observatory Project and TMT Mid-Level Facility Project, Maunakea, Ka'ohe Ahupua'a, Hāmākua District, Hawai'i Island*. Cultural Surveys Hawai'i, Inc., Feb. 2010.

Smith, Richard Gordon. "The Procession of Ghosts." *Ancient Tales and Folk-Lore of Japan*. Bracken Books, 1986.

Smith, Ronald Vivian. "Creatures of the Night." *India Today*, 29 Dec. 2009, www.indiatoday.in/magazine/supplement/story/2009122 1-creatures-of-the-night-741510-2009-12-11.

Sommer, Anthony. "State Seeks Permit to Revive Kauai Airfield." *Honolulu Star-Bulletin*, 18 Mar. 2002, pp. A3, https://www.newspapers.com/image/274510863/. Accessed 2 Mar. 2020.

Sterling, Elspeth P., and Catherine C. Summers. *Sites of Oahu*. Bishop Museum Press, 1978.

Stevens Poire, Napua. "Night Marchers Scared Her." *The Honolulu Advertiser*, 31 Oct. 1971, pp. C7, https://www.newspapers.com/image/261095826/. Accessed 2 Mar. 2020.

Taylor, Lois. "Spook Stories." *Honolulu Star-Bulletin*, 21 Oct. 1972, pp. F1, https://www.newspapers.com/image/271519216/. Accessed 2 Mar. 2020.

Thrum, Thomas G. "Heiaus and Heiau Sites throughout the Hawaiian Islands." *Hawaiian Almanac and Annual for 1907*, vol. 33, 1906, pp. 36–48., http://hdl.handle.net/10524/32457.

Thrum, Thomas G. "Tales from the Temples (with plans)." *Hawaiian Almanac and Annual for 1907*, vol. 33, 1906, pp. 49–69., http://hdl.handle.net/10524/32457.

Thrum, Thomas G. "Heiaus and Heiau Sites throughout the Hawaiian Islands." *Hawaiian Almanac and Annual for 1908*, vol. 34, 1907, pp. 38–47., http://hdl.handle.net/10524/32462.

Thrum, Thomas G. "Tales from the Temples with Plans and illustrations." *Hawaiian Almanac and Annual for 1908*, vol. 34, 1907, pp. 48–78., http://hdl.handle.net/10524/32462.

Thrum, Thomas G. "Heiaus; their kinds, constructions, ceremonies, etc." *Hawaiian Almanac and Annual for 1910*, vol. 35, 1909, pp. 53–71., http://hdl.handle.net/10524/32834.

Walk, Devin. "The Fort De Chartes Ghost Procession." *Memories of the Prairie*, Memories of the Prairie, 19 Feb. 2019, www.memoriesoftheprairie.com/blog/2019/2/19/the-fort-de-chartes-ghost-procession.

Weaver, Zofia. "Our History." *Society for Psychical Research*, www.spr.ac.uk/home.

Westervelt, William Drake. *Hawaiian Legends of Ghosts and Ghost-Gods*. Charles E. Tuttle Company, 1964.

"What Is the Parapsychological Association?" *The Parapsychological Association*, 25 Sept. 2010, parapsych.org/articles/1/1/what_is_the_parapsychological.aspx.

Wichman, Juliet Rice. *Hawaiian Planting Traditions*. Honolulu Star-Bulletin, 1931.

"Will Investigate the Psychic." *The Maui News*, 12 Dec. 1919, p. 2, chroniclingamerica.loc.gov/data/batches/hihouml_granite_ver01/data/sn82014689/00237289936/1919121201/0417.pdf.

Willis, Koko, and Pali Jae Lee. *Tales from the Night Rainbow Mo'olelo o Na Pō Makole: the Story of a Woman, a People, and an Island*. Night Rainbow Publishing Co., 1990.

Withington, Antoinette. *Hawaiian Tapestry*. Harper & Bros, 1937.

About the Illustrator

Alika Spahn Naihe is a kanaka maoli digital artist and game designer. Born and raised on the island of Oʻahu, Hawaiʻi, Alika spent much of his childhood sketching and doodling on any pieces of paper he could find, whether at home, in class, or at his grandparents' house, where he spent most of his time. As a teenager, he saw the art of Solomon Enos - the Kamapuaʻa series - in a Hawaiian Airlines in-flight magazine that sparked what would become a deep fascination with Hawaiian mythology and the art inspired by it. After working in various occupations - from kitchen prep to baking cookies to landscaping to becoming a journeyman electrician at Pearl Harbor Naval Shipyard - he decided to make his lifelong hobby of art his life's work.

Alika has a design and apparel business, Hauʻoli Art, where he creates art and clothing inspired by the Hawaiian culture. Alika is also a part-owner of Theorycraftist Games along with Jeffrey Vierra and Jack Hobbs, where he is the head artist and leads the manufacturing and production of their games. Together, Jeffrey, Jack, and Alika teach an after-school game design class at Nānākuli High School under the PALS program.

You can connect with the artist at the following links:

www.hauoliart.com
www.theorycraftist.com
Instagram: @hauoli_art_alika
Email: alika@hauoliart.com

About the Authors

Best known as "Hawaii's Ghost Guy," Master Storyteller Lopaka Kapanui, has been scaring people and sharing Hawaii's stories for more than twenty-five years. A native Hawaiian born and raised on Oʻahu and spending his childhood vacations on Hawaiʻi Island and Maui, Lopaka learned about his family's history, customs and protocol, which were passed down to him in the traditional Hawaiian way, through moʻolelo, from mouth to ear, sitting at the foot of his Mother and his Aunty as they related the lessons to him. He learned the significance of the proper prayers to offer in ceremonial blessings, to enter or leave a sacred place, to ask for protection or forgiveness, or before gathering greenery in depths of a Hawaiian forest, and the importance of intent. Additionally, he was taught that the responsibility which would come with what he was going to inherit would have to, one day, be passed down. As a Master Storyteller, Lopaka has received a special citation from the Hawaiʻi State Legislature in 2020 for perpetuating and celebrating local culture, history, language, and folklore through storytelling and knowledge of these Islands' history and legends.

Born in Denver, Colorado and raised in a military family, Tanya Kapanui had the privilege of living in Colorado, Texas, and Germany before making Hawaiʻi, where her parents were born and raised, her home for the last thirty years. As a lifelong horror aficionado, Tanya's interest in the supernatural was established at a very young age, but it wasn't until she was older that her interests expanded to native legends like the Filipino aswang and the Hawaiian moʻo. The last three years have been dedicated to intense research on the huakaʻi pō. When she's not reading, researching hauntings and ghost stories, or running their ghost tour business, Tanya can be found spending time with their amazing grandchildren.

Together, the couple runs Mysteries of Hawaiʻi, sharing some of Hawaii's scariest stories with the world.

www.Mysteries-of-Hawaii.com

Made in the USA
Las Vegas, NV
16 September 2023

77662168R00109